Purchased 7/27/85
at "Cabbages and Kings"
Kathy Simmons Summer employment

10.⁹⁵

Seasons of the SALT MARSH

BOOKS BY DAVID ALAN GATES
Oyster Propogation (1964)
Ecology of the Oyster Pond Estuarine System,
   Chatham, Massachusetts (1970)
Biological Survey of Pleasant Bay,
   Chatham, Massachusetts (1971)

BOOKS ILLUSTRATED BY EDWARD AND MARCIA NORMAN
The Winter Beach
The Atlantic Shore
Seaweeds of Cape Cod and the Islands
The Sandy Shore
The Rocky Shore
A Sampler of Wayside Herbs
A Beachcomber's Botany

ILLUSTRATED BY

Edward and Marcia Norman

Contents

David Alan Gates

Seasons of the SALT MARSH

THE CHATHAM PRESS   OLD GREENWICH, CONNECTICUT

This book is dedicated to
those who count the most:
Mim, Glenn, Garry, Gregory and Gailynn

ACKNOWLEDGEMENTS
My gratitude to Mr. John M. Gray, Chairman of the English Department at Nauset
Regional High School, Eastham, Massachusetts, for technical and general assistance in
preparation of the original manuscript.
  A special note of thanks to Edward and Marcia Norman whose persistant encourage-
ment has seen me through this literary endeavor.

— D.A.G.

Library of Congress Catalog Card No.: 74-27956
ISBN 85699-121-X

DESIGNED BY CHRISTOPHER HARRIS

Printed in the U.S.A. by the Murray Printing Co.

Introduction

A salt marsh is a relatively flat, low-lying portion of the coast-line, alternatively called a wetland, swamp, or tidal marsh. In a salt marsh, the land is partially submerged at high tide and is inhabited by vegetation that has adapted to living in a highly saline environment.

The inland limit of a salt marsh is generally controlled by the height of the water during the high "spring" tides which occur roughly twice each month when the sun and moon are in line with our planet. These tides are called "spring" due to the fact that at this time water seems to spring from the earth; the name has nothing to do with the spring season. On the east coast of the United States, ocean tides are of the semidiurnal type, meaning there are two high and two low tides each day with only very slight daily difference between consecutive high or low water as the tides progress from neap to spring and back.

Salt marshes may form behind sandspits, barrier beaches and islands or within harbors, inlets and bays, where protection from the destructive power of pounding surf is assured. They are found along our entire eastern coast from Eastport, Maine, to the semi-tropical regions of Florida, where mangrove swamps replace them.

The size and shape of these transitional zones between land and sea are generally determined by land contour and the amount of sediment available from the waters.

More often than not, marshes will form along estuaries — bodies of water in the coastal zone where fresh water from rivers and streams meets the sea. From these sources come the essential minerals that have been leached from the land and the detritus (decaying organic matter) and sediments that have been carried downstream during the river's tumultuous journey to the sea. The meeting of fresh and salt water creates a mixing action that holds these materials in suspension, making them available as nutrients for the phytoplankton — microscopic plants that form the base of the wetland food chain.

The marsh, together with its meandering tidal creeks and estuary, is a geological, physical and biological complex known as a marsh ecosystem, a number of which exist within the eastern coastal zone. In the maritime regions of Canada, salt marshes are relatively limited in size, being confined to small pockets along protected coasts. Here the dominant marsh vegetation is goose grass *(Puccinellia maritima)* which, like all northern flora, has a short growing season. Fine silt and red mud characterize the marshes of the Bay of Fundy, where vegetation is sparse. The glaciated coastal zone of the United States from Maine to upper New Jersey has relatively small marshes with a peat base and a dominant vegetation of the short salt-meadow grass *Spartina patens.* Along the eastern shore of Cape May in southern New Jersey and continuing down to the southern limits of Pamlico Bay in North Carolina, the basal material of the marshes has a mineral content typical of unglaciated coasts. Marshes here are much more extensive than those further north, but the fine salt-meadow grass still dominates.

The four southern Atlantic coast states, North and South Carolina, Georgia, and Florida, have approximately one and a half million acres of salt marshes, or seventy per cent of the east coast total. From Cape Lookout, North Carolina, south to the middle of Florida, the marshes take on a new character. *Spartina alterniflora*, the tall, coarse salt-water cord grass, replaces the finer, shorter salt-meadow grass as the dominant vegetation. The tide has a greater range here, resulting in more extensive flooding of these lowlands, for which reason the drainage system of the marshes is more highly developed. There are fewer tide pools on the marsh itself, and the meandering tidal creeks often measure many miles in length, resembling small rivers. Many are deep enough to be navigable by small boats, making them favorite hunting and fishing sites.

Throughout the year tidal marshes are subjected to a variety of environmental conditions. Being part land and part sea, they experience the best and worst of both. All marsh animals must adjust to the twice-daily flooding by the tide and the wide fluctuations in salinity that may occur as a result of heavy rains during the ebb tide. Each season presents its own particular problems to the marsh organisms, though the inhabitants of the southern marshes do not experience extremes in weather as do their counterparts in more northerly marshes.

Severe winters in the North bring freezing temperatures, sleet, hail, snow and ice. Tidal creeks often freeze over, and ice cakes may move across the surface of the marsh. This is the time when the food supply is almost nonexistent, and only the keenest hunting prowess will keep a marsh animal from starvation. Although the marsh then offers an inhospitable environment to the few plants and animals that make it their home, nature has provided these organisms with a multitude of mechanisms to deal with unfavorable conditions. Biological clocks enable some of the animals to time their food-gathering activities to coincide with the never-ending pulse of the tide — such as the air-breathing snails that climb the spartina stems twice a day to keep from being drowned by the incoming tide. Each marsh inhabitant adjusts in its own unique and fascinating way.

Seasons of the Salt Marsh provides an account of how the marsh plants and animals cope with the day-to-day problems of existence in an ever-fluctuating environment. The first chapter deals in general with the formation of the typical marshes in the eastern coastal zone of the United States; fauna and flora of the entire east coast are included, although it must be kept in mind that the further south one goes, the less effect the seasons have.

The variations in the life of the marsh of a specific nature are examined in the season-by-season chapters that follow. Following the chapter on the winter season, the far-reaching importance of marshes and the role they play in our economy are considered, including the historical and present uses of marsh fauna and flora, concluding with a plea for the exercise of carefully weighed foresight in the use of these delicate wetlands.

The final section of the book is an illustrated appendix of the most common indigenous species of plants and animals of our eastern coastal marshes. It is intended to serve as a field guide for those who wish to identify the amazing creatures who live within the confines of these fragile wetlands.

The Formation of a Marsh

When the great ice sheet called the Laurentide Glacier released its heavy grip and slowly retreated northward, the landscape it left behind underwent considerable alteration. As the ice melted, the sand, silt, clay, boulders and debris that had been scraped and dragged along the coastal plain were deposited at the southern limit of the glacier, forming the terminal moraine east of New York City now called Long Island. As this process continued, other moraines were deposited, creating Martha's Vineyard and Nantucket Islands and Cape Cod.

Coincidental with the melting process, some ten thousand years ago, crustal movement of the coastal area, coupled with the rising seas, created other features that are evident along our entire eastern seaboard. Maine acquired a rockbound coast similar to Norway's with its fjords. River systems from New Hampshire to the Chesapeake Bay area became inundated by the sea, giving rise to major estuaries. From Virginia to Florida, a long string of barrier islands was formed.

Wind, rain, and the ever-pounding sea gnawed away, continually altering the landscape and its fauna and flora. The scrub oak and pitch pine growth that today covers much of the coastal plain replaced majestic forests of cedar, beech, birch, hickory and maple. Longshore currents were instrumental in removing tons of sand along the beaches; as erosion occurred in one area, accretion, the building up of the land, took place in another. In this way, spits, sandbars and barrier beaches were formed, cutting off small bays, lagoons and inlets from the force of the sea. Sediments carried up with the tides and washed from land by streams and rivers were deposited in the bays and inlets. With each gentle creep of the tide, more and more particles of fine silt and clay were laid down until gradually the land beneath the ocean rose and the mud flats came up to the level of the sea at high water.

In geological time, the salt marshes of our glaciated coast are relative newcomers — probably only around three thousand years old. Some of the marshes further south are even younger, but most are older and well established. Regardless of when they were formed, most marshes were created in a similar pattern.

Wave action is limited on the mud flat because there is little or no slope to the land. Organisms that take up residence here need no special holdfasts or adhesive bases as they do on rocky coasts, though in other ways the mud flat still presents them with a hostile environment. Because it is exposed at low tide and subject to rainfall and out-flowing streams, the salinity of its waters can change from salt to fresh in a matter of minutes, while in the northern coastal region temperatures on a sun-baked flat may reach 90°F. or more and drop swiftly to 50°F. when the tide flows in.

Other than the microscopic algae (diatoms and dinoflagellates), eelgrass *(Zostera marina)*, one of the few flowering plants able to survive in a completely submerged environment, was the first to help stabilize the mud flats and form marshes. During slack tide, sediments in the water dropped out of suspension, were deposited on the bottom near the edge of the flats and trapped by the roots of the submerged eelgrass. In this manner, tidal flats increased in size and the eelgrass community spread, creating a more permanent structure.

In time, the mud flat became inhabited by countless marine worms, mollusks, crabs, and myriad other organisms. As each lived out its life, its organic remains became part of the mud, enriching it with nutrients.

Exposed at low tide, the flats were visited by migrating birds that may have been the carriers of seeds from other areas, though most seeds had no chance of survival on land that was flooded twice each day. But the warm, moist mud of summer, harboring organic detritus from the eelgrass and animals of the flats, did supply hospitality for a very special seed — that of the spartina grass — and germination quickly followed when these seeds were deposited. It is also possible that fragments containing rooted spartina grass broke off from established marshes, washed up on the virgin mud of newly forming flats and took hold and spread as their rhizomes pushed through the nutrient mud. Soon the backbone of a new marsh had been established.

Of the thousands of different kinds of plants known, spartina is one of the very few whose seeds can germinate in this unfriendly environment. In the course of its evolution, spartina developed a series of special gland cells that regulate the delicate balance between salt and water, a necessity for any plant that is to survive in this partially submerged marine world. Propagation by rhizomes enabled the plant to persist even when its tops were sheared off by the winter ice floes of a northern marsh.

Spartina grasses are now the dominant vegetation of most marshes, and it is upon this photosynthesizing plant that the marsh animals depend. While eelgrass lives on the outermost reaches of the mud flat in the deeper water and is at all times completely submerged, spartina thrives on the flat itself, where its roots are submerged twice a day at each high tide. Probably for hundreds of years, *Spartina alterniflora* dominated each new marsh area and, together with the constantly entering mud and silt, formed a thick deposit of peat. This process continued until a second type of spartina grass became established — *Spartina patens*. We find this grass, called marsh hay, further from the water's edge and higher up on the marsh.

The species *Spartina alterniflora* and *Spartina patens* differ greatly from each other in their physical appearance. *Spartina alterniflora*, or salt-water cord grass, is much larger — its leaves may be up to one half inch or more in width at the base and may grow to a height of over six feet along the marsh creeks. *Spartina patens* is a much finer grass and may grow to a foot or so in locations where the roots will be submerged only during spring tides. *Spartina patens* grows so thickly and forms such tight root-mats that competition from other plants is practically eliminated, though spike grass *(Distichlis)*, similar in appearance to *Spartina patens*, may also occupy scattered areas on the higher levels of the marsh.

Still further back towards the dry land, where drainage is poor and the area may be quite saline from evaporating salt water, will be found another common botanical inhabitant — the fleshy, succulent-stemmed glasswort *(Salicornia)*, which used to be pickled and eaten as a delicacy.

The upland limit of the marsh itself is considered to be bounded by the *Juncus*, or black grass, zone. Here sea water will go only when storms coincide with spring tides. Beyond is the transitional zone, which receives only occasional salt spray during storms and supports its own unique community of plants and animals.

A bird's-eye view of a marsh would present a mosaic of distinct and differentiated grasses, tidal pools and the meandering streams which serve as drainage channels and which are formed as the flooded marsh gives up its water to the ebbing tide. The stronger the outgoing tide, the more erosion occurs. Over the years the sea will cut a multitude of such drainage creeks. As the marsh builds up through the accumulation of silt from the ocean and organic matter from the marsh itself, these creeks can attain a considerable width and depth, permitting passage for many good-sized fish at high tide.

Spartina alterniflora takes up residence along these tidal creeks, and on the mud-banks a host of animals dig in. The ribbed mussel is especially abundant in the substrate at the base of the spartina. At low tide, one can observe thousands of fiddler crabs wandering away from the safety of their burrows in search of food.

Tidal pools on the marsh itself develop where there are irregularities in the height of the land and drainage is poor or nonexistent. During an extreme spring tide, the marsh may be completely flooded; as the tide ebbs, many of these pools, or pans as they are sometimes called, remain flooded. They may support a variety of life, including many small fish such as the mummichog, killifish, and minnow. Depending upon the salinity of the trapped water, widgeon grass *(Ruppia maritima)* may grow quite profusely in these pools.

Thus these wetlands called salt marshes can be identified by their dominant vegetation. Differences in marshes are due in part to weather conditions and the ability of plants to tolerate these conditions. In the North, Canadian coastal marshes are composed mostly of the grass *Puccinellia.* In New England and the Middle Atlantic coastal regions down to North Carolina, *Spartina alterniflora* and *Spartina patens* dominate, with the latter making up the bulk of the marsh grasses. Further south, the marshes are almost exclusively *Spartina alterniflora,* while on the coast of southern Florida, the marsh gives way to mangrove swamps.

Compared to the extensive marshes of the southern states, the New England marshes are relatively small, but in spite of their size, of all the coastal marshes in the United States they are

the most beautiful and best preserved. No matter what its size, the coastal wetland is always bustling with life and always in a state of dynamic equilibrium with the environment — abounding in splendid colors throughout the year, everchanging from day to day and from season to season.

This then is the year of the salt marsh.

Spring
The Time of Awakening

March twenty-first, the spring equinox, is the day the sun's rays are directly perpendicular to the equator. This is the official beginning of the season that ushers in new life. But nature does not change her dress abruptly — there are still many days ahead that will resemble winter. On the northern marshes more snow may fall, northeast storms will still batter the fragile coast, and ice may be slow to melt.

In the southern marshes changes are more subtle and, with the exception of migratory birds that stop by on their way to their nesting ground, life goes on as usual. The new grasses have long ago begun to grow and last year's brown spartina has given way to fresh green shoots during the winter. By the time spring officially arrives, the southern marshes resemble the green carpets that in the North may be seen only in late spring and summer.

Although they come slowly, there are many perceptible changes. The sun now rides a longer course across the sky and the noonday shadows begin to shorten. Winds gradually shift around to a more southerly direction, bringing with them a warming trend. Buds shed the waxy scales that have protected their delicate tissue through the winter and begin to grow.

The rays of the sun slowly warm the land, and snow begins to melt on the mountain peaks. Along the Appalachian range, the oldest chain of mountains in the United States, the melted snow starts its tumultuous journey to the sea. From Canada to Alabama the mighty rivers of our east coast — the Connecticut, Hudson, Delaware, Potomac, Susquehanna, Rappahannock, Pamlico, Neuse, Congaree and Savannah, plus a thousand tributaries — gather minerals and organic detritus from the land and carry it down to Atlantic shores.

The high spring tides flood the marsh, and ice cakes and frost give way to clear fresh water. Detritus that has lain beneath the ice and snow all winter is released and spread by icy waters that carry it around the marsh into tidal creeks and bays. Over half of this nutrient will enter the food web of the deep-water marine world; the remainder will be consumed by the marsh-dwellers themselves.

Algae along the mud creek-banks of the marsh respond to these additives, for even green plants require certain metabolites for their food-making processes. In springtime we see plankton blooms along the coastal estuaries as winter releases its seal on the land.

Not only are the microscopic plants and animals the beneficiaries of this added food, but many benthic and pelagic marine forms now make their way inshore for fresh nourishment. And so the melting of the ice and snow triggers a series of events that will continue through the year. The winter flounder, or blackback, which has bred in the coastal region during the winter, now leaves the marsh waters and heads out to sea, only to be replaced by the summer flounder that migrates in from the cold ocean depths.

The remains of the previous year's marsh plants are carried out of the creeks and into the bay to be spun into the food web as the larval forms of crabs, snails, worms, starfish and copepods consume the nutrient and pass it on as they themselves are eaten.

Everywhere life is beginning anew — spring peepers herald the coming of the new season. The air becomes filled with the mating calls of birds — the males are busy staking out their territory and enticing the females to accept their favors. Trees bud, sap flows and the grass turns green — new life is evident.

Spring ushers in a new life cycle for the marsh plants. Exposed seeds that have lain upon the marsh floor throughout the winter need only the warmth of the sun and the fresh spring rain to emerge from their seed coats and push their root structure into the soft marsh mud. Though most seeds of the spartina grasses are eaten by birds or are washed into the tidal estuaries, their underground stems, the rhizomes, are perennial, and during early spring, new, soft green shoots begin to emerge through last year's spartina culms.

Black grass *(Juncus)*, evident on the border of the marsh along the entire east coast, is indicative of fresh water inflow. The southern species, *Juncus Roemerianus*, and the northern, *J. Gerardi*, are among the first plants to appear in the spring, at which time they will resemble the green grasses. Later in the year, the green of chlorophyll will give way to the gray-black hue from which the plant derives its common name.

Inhabiting the same general niche as *Spartina patens* is the perennial spike grass *(Distichlis spicata)*. New fresh green shoots appear in compact colonies that push up from their creeping, underground stem. The previous year's growth is easily distinguished by its curled leaf-blade.

Three species of *Salicornia* are common on the marshes; all are rather short and fleshy and have an almost translucent stem. The unbranched perennial *S. virginica*, known as woody glasswort because of its woody stem, is found growing in sandy soil on the higher parts of the marsh. *S. europaea* and the taller *S. Bigelovii* are annual species, both having branched, succulent, jointed stems. The annual species are often found in low-lying

depressions of the marsh where evaporation has increased the salinity to a degree much greater than the normal three and a half per cent in sea water, since *Salicornia* seeds have the unusual characteristic of being able to germinate in highly saline waters.

Low-lying areas of the marsh that do not drain properly or remain filled as the sea recedes are known as ruppia pools, so named as the habitat of widgeon grass *(Ruppia maritima)*, whose common name derives from the fact that it is a favorite food of the widgeon duck. The water in these pools may vary greatly in salt content, but they still support their own community of organisms, including small minnows, killifish and an occasional blue crab *(Callinectes sapidus)*. These transient visitors will leave on the next high tide, when water once again covers the marsh and offers them an avenue of escape.

Sea lavender, or marsh rosemary *(Limonium carolinianum)*, which has large green leaves growing close to the ground and in late summer produces miniature lavender blossoms on its woody, highly branched stalk, is at home on the upland borders of the marsh where the soil is still salty.

Each marsh plant is adapted to its own particular home. Where fresh water flows onto the marsh, zones of gradually varying salinity are set up that favor one plant or another. In fresh-to-brackish areas we find slough, salt-reed grass, wild rye, soft rush, chairmaker's rush and salt-marsh bulrush. Cat-tails and reeds are common here, as are orach, plantain, sand spurrey and salt-marsh aster. Ladies' tresses, marsh pinks, swamp rose mallow, knotweed, milkwort and goldenrod grow well in this transitional zone between salt and fresh. Upland are the horned rush, sedge, slender-leaved goldenrod and the groundsel tree.

Flowering plants are not conspicuous in the spring marsh — nearly all are in their infantile stage and resemble any of a number of green grasses. In their reproduction period during summer or autumn, many will have brightly colored floral parts.

From southern Greenland to New Jersey, the early seaside plantain *(Plantago juncoides* var. *decipiens)* is one of the first plants of the marsh to flower. This deep-rooted perennial with fleshy, narrow linear leaves will send up a stalk in early June with small, off-white flowers which lead off a parade of colors that will continue all summer and into the fall.

Nearly every animal phylum is represented on the marsh, from the lowly sponges and worms to the highest mammals. Each is found in its own specific habitat going about its appointed tasks. The quahogs, clams, worms and even the small minnows and killifish that have spent the winter under the protective cover of mud begin to stir as the warm rays of the sun penetrate the marsh.

One animal that has withstood the rigors of winter exposed to the elements is the inedible ribbed mussel *(Modiolus demissus),* one of the most abundant of the marsh animals. Thousands

of these organisms are wedged in, side by side, at the base of the *Spartina alterniflora* in the intertidal zone. A close scrutiny of this animal brings to mind Gulliver as he lay on the beach at Lilliput tied down to the sand by tiny ropes — for the mussel is tied down by tiny threads secreted by a special gland in the animal's atrophied foot. There it will remain with the pointed end of its shell facing toward the sea, the better to withstand the force of the waves.

In the economy of the marsh and estuarine water, the mussel plays a vital role. Since he is a filter feeder, water passes through the animal at a rate of three to four quarts per hour, with organic particles being strained out for food. The abundance of these particles creates an excess, which is stuck together by mucus and deposited on the marsh as pseudofeces rich in phosphates which will, in turn, provide nutrient for other animals.

The raccoon, or "a-ra-kun-em" as the Indians called him

(meaning "he who scratches with his hands"), is found in almost every environment. This nocturnal omnivore will sometimes build his nest of spartina grasses up on the higher levels of the marsh. He takes a back seat to no one for the title of chief scavenger. The raccoon will eat just about anything it can find, including fish, crabs, clams, oysters, mice and frogs, and will even resort to stealing eggs from the nests of marsh birds. It has a reputation of being a fastidious creature and is sometimes seen scratching up a helpless mollusk from the marsh bed, then washing the food in water before eating it. Raccoons do not hibernate, but may take extended naps of several days in cold weather, though on warm sunny days, even in winter, you may see them scavenging. They breed in February, and by the first part of spring can be seen in and around the marsh looking for anything nutritious to bring back to the nest.

Hermit crabs *(Pagurus pollicaris)* can be seen laboriously walking about on the marsh creek-bed with the discarded shells of various gastropods on their backs. As the hermit crab grows it must abandon one shell and seek out another. Often two crabs compete for the same living quarters, and as nature demands, the weaker contestant must seek another shell. Occasionally a hermit crab living peacefully within a shell is literally pulled from his house by a more aggressive one. If you have patience, you may be rewarded by the sight of several of these crabs in a group trying on each other's shells for size. When a crab finds one that feels comfortable, little hooks on its abdominal segments will fasten it securely to the shell until it is time to seek new quarters once again.

Warming waters of the creeks and tide pools on the marsh bring new life and activity to the mummichogs, minnows and banded killifish that have been relatively inactive through the winter. The waters are alive with crangon and copepods, whose numbers increase greatly following the phytoplankton blooms.

Along the coast, the American lobster *(Homarus americanus)* in the North and the spiny lobster *(Panulirus argus)* in the South begin their annual migrations to coastal areas to take advantage of the newly increased food supply. Some will remain in shallow inlets and bays for the summer, but many *Homarus* continue up to the coasts of Maine and Newfoundland to reproduce before heading back to deeper water in the fall.

Menhaden come in from the deep in enormous schools to feed on the snapping shrimp that now appear in increasing numbers in tidal estuaries. In southern New England these fish spawn in early June. Further north they may spawn twice a year, in the spring and again in the fall. In the coastal regions off Maryland and Virginia, the menhaden spawn around October, while in Georgia and Florida spawning is delayed until winter. In the North, cod *(Gadus callaris)* may follow the newly spawned fish in from the sea, for this delicious herring is one of their staple foods.

Alewives will pass through tidal creeks on their way to headland waters to spawn. The adults return to the sea almost immediately, while the young follow a few weeks later. Shad, mullet, striped bass and flounder are but a few of the many fish that can be seen swimming in marsh waters. It has been estimated that over half of all commercially valuable fish and shellfish spend part of their lives within the environs of a salt marsh.

The southern, or lined, periwinkle *(Littorina irrorata)*, like most snails, is a vegetarian. It is often seen climbing the spartina stems and scraping off the residue of plant detritus that the tide has left behind. Although originating in the South, this species has spread from the Gulf of Mexico up the east coast as far north as Massachusetts. Unlike its northern cousin *L. littorea*, which has a preference for more wave action, *L. irrorata* relishes the quiet waters of the marsh.

On a marsh at low tide, pick up some of the grass and debris lying on the marsh floor and you will see hundreds of tiny gastropod snails. This is the salt-marsh snail, *Melampus*. Unlike other snails of the marsh, it is an air breather, a characteristic that would seem to inhibit its living in an intertidal zone. But a built-in biological clock tells *Melampus* exactly when the tide is about to rise; a few minutes before the sea flows in, all these snails start their twice-a-day journey up the stems of the spartina grasses. As the water rises, so does *Melampus*. Should the water cover the stem, the snail can usually hold its breath long enough for the tide to recede. These snails breed in the springtime, and their eggs hatch into free-floating larvae which will depend upon tide, currents and wind to deposit them at some favorable spot.

Insects are well represented in the marsh — mosquitoes, beetles, flies, spiders, plant hoppers, crickets and grasshoppers. Most will spend the winter in the egg, larva or nymph stage and emerge in the spring. Tidal pools of the marsh are often covered with wigglers (the larval form of the mosquito), their breathing tubes projecting to the water's surface. These larvae make excellent food for fish, birds and predacious insects. The larvae of greenhead flies have fleshy lobes extending from each segment to aid in crawling. The maggots live in the upper surface of the marsh mud. As adults during the summer, greenheads are probably the most obnoxious creatures of the marsh. People who are attacked by these flies while picnicking on nearby beaches may be interested to know that it is the female of the species who must consume a blood meal to insure proper metabolism of her reproductive organs; the male is generally harmless, being content to feed off flowers.

Insects may seem to be nothing but a nuisance, but in the economy of the marsh they play the important role of eating and being eaten as energy is passed along the food chain. Insect life is kept in check by the gulls, swallows, wrens, sparrows, willets and rails that migrate in during the spring.

The nymphs of grasshoppers and crickets emerge from their egg cases and set about satisfying their voracious appetites by eating the tender young shoots of the spartina and other marsh plants. The large black American field cricket *(Acheta assimilis)* lays its eggs in the fall, and the nymphs emerge the following spring, molt five or six times, develop wings and reproduce. Crickets, more numerous on northern marshes than grasshoppers, are the musicians of the marsh. Their sound production is almost exclusively a male trait and involves rubbing together two parts of the body, the pitch changing with the temperature.

At first glance, the barnacle *(Balanus balanoides)* looks like a mollusk, but his larval form is a giveaway that he belongs instead to the crustacean group. Barnacles are fairly common around the salt marsh, making their homes on some hard object — a rock, a clam shell or the back of a horseshoe crab resembling a small volcano with its steep white calcareous sides and having a top that can open and close by movement of some of these plates, the barnacle can protrude his appendages and scoop water containing food into the interior of his shell. Except during a free-swimming larval stage, the barnacle is a sessile organism that remains attached to one spot throughout its life. Being a hermaphrodite, but unable to fertilize itself, this creature has a problem in reproduction. If two barnacles are close enough together, a tube to transfer sperm reaches out from one to the other, thereby insuring a new generation. But a lone barnacle, too far from its nearest neighbor, is condemned to live out his life as a celibate.

Perhaps the most interesting animals of the marsh are the fiddler crabs *(Uca* sp.). They are late risers and usually do not come up from their tunnels along the creek-banks until the middle of May, when the sun's penetrating rays have warmed the marsh. Even in South Carolina and Georgia, the fiddler is inactive during the winter.

The higher forms of marsh animals consist of fish, reptiles, birds and mammals — birds being the most common. The true marsh birds, those that actually live and nest within the marsh, are few in number. Marsh hawks *(Circus cyaneus hudsonius)* nest on high spots along the marsh; the clapper rail *(Rallus longirostris)*, which has a body "as thin as a rail," is sometimes seen running between the spartina strands, but generally keeps very prudently hidden from view. The clapper builds its nest in areas of dense *Spartina alterniflora.* In this same general part of the marsh will be found the nests of the long-bulled marsh wren *(Tematodytes palustris).* Along the marsh creek, also among the *Spartina alterniflora* but upland, we find the home of the small seaside sparrow *(Ammospiza maritima). Spartina patens* is the nesting site of the sharp-tailed sparrow *(A. caudacuta).*

Other birds, not true salt-marsh dwellers, occasionally build their nests on the marsh. These include the American bittern *(Botaurus lentiginosus)* — normally a fresh-water marsh inhabitant usually found in the South — red-wing blackbirds, black ducks, short-eared owls and grackles. Birds that use the marsh as a feeding ground include ducks, geese, plovers, curlews, herons, sandpipers, rails and gulls.

The true marsh birds have special nesting problems. Although a small nest hidden in hundreds of acres of marsh grass would seem to be well protected, the rise and fall of the tide is a constant threat, and to guard against flooding, nests are usually built off the marsh floor. Predation is an ever-present danger — raccoons, skunks and mink often raid nests to suck the eggs. To compensate for this inevitable loss, many marsh birds — for instance, the clapper rail — will often breed twice a season, laying as many as a dozen eggs each time so that enough chicks will survive to maintain the species.

The cousin of the clapper, the sora *(Porzana carolina)* is the most common rail in North America. This small, rather plump

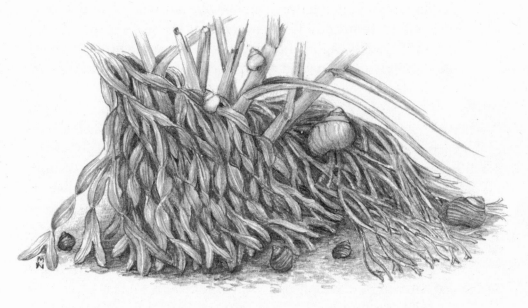

BARRY X BALL

7/28/85

"...THIS DAY SHALT THOU BE
WITH ME IN PARADISE."

gray-brown bird lives in both fresh- and salt-water marshes along the coast, but rarely in the North. It winters in southern marshes and occasionally may be seen emerging along the creek-banks to seek a meal of insects.

Ducks feed on aquatic plants and fish and only a few of them actually nest on the marsh. Black ducks and mallards spend the winters in protected harbors and coves, but when spring arrives they will mate and build their nests along the edges of the marsh.

In the warm waters of the creek, the wading birds — green, blue, and night herons and egrets — can be seen up to their knees in water, waiting patiently for a minnow to swim by.

The birds of prey are ever present — osprey and fishhawks looking for a meal of bass or menhaden. The marsh hawk circles high above, ever alert for a newly hatched chick or a mouse.

An early spring migrant is the greater yellow-legs *(Totanus melanoleucus)* on its way to Labrador and the Hudson Bay regions where it will nest. Returning along the Atlantic flyway in the autumn, this large sandpiper will be seen standing in marsh creeks on its long, bright yellow legs watching the waters intently for an unsuspecting fish. It winters from Pamlico Sound in North Carolina to the St. John's River in northern Florida.

The common tern *(Sterna hirundo)* arrives in April or May from its winter quarters in Brazil. After mating, it will nest along the coast. Three weeks later, the female lays two or three pale-brown spotted eggs which will hatch in about three more weeks. The chicks are ready for flying in July but practice their fine art for several weeks before heading back to South America. In two or three years they too will return to our Atlantic coast. Terns will only eat live food and are often seen skimming over the water, head bent, eyes fixed upon the surface. Once it spots a fish, the tern will put on its air brakes and plunge headlong into the ocean water, often disappearing from view entirely, only to reappear with a small fish in its bill.

The male marsh wren *(Telmatodytes palustris)* arrives early in May and at once spends a couple of weeks in the construction business, building a number of nests which he will proudly display when the female flies in two weeks later. This building behavior is probably a courting maneuver to entice a female into setting up housekeeping but, in spite of all the male's work, the pair will build still another nest in which the female will lay her eggs.

Most birds of the salt-marsh areas are only transients, staying for varying lengths of time on their way north in the spring or south in the autumn. They stop by a place in their migratory patterns only to feed. We simply do not know why birds migrate, although many theories have been advanced to explain this annual phenomenon. It has been suggested that all birds were originally tropical species and as their population became overcrowded in those regions some flew to the higher latitudes in the spring, were driven back by the arrival of winter and thereby set up a migratory pattern. Another theory holds that birds were distributed over a wide geographic range but when climatic conditions changed, the glaciers drove the birds south. As the glaciers retreated, a larger and larger number of hospitable habitats for nesting became available in the North, setting up migratory reproductive patterns. Other hypotheses, relating to the influence of available food, the length of daylight and even a relationship between continental drift and flight patterns, have been advanced. Since all the theories thus far proposed have serious flaws, it may be that the answer lies in a combination of two or more. Scientific scrutiny will undoubtedly yield further clues as time goes on.

Summer
The Time of Growth

Days grow longer, coastal waters warm and activities speed up. For the babies of the marsh it is a time of growing and maturing, a time of challenges and fear, of learning behavior patterns that will insure long life — a time when parental guidance must be strictly adhered to and all energy must be directed toward survival.

As the tide rises, marsh birds double their efforts at hunting small crabs and crawling insects that have taken refuge atop the spartina grasses. Their caloric intake must increase as instinct informs the parents that there are more mouths to feed in the nest. Soft, downy nesting chicks belie their eventual status in society; the helpless, white hatchlings of the hawk soon become the feared dark-winged predators of the marsh.

Early summer is also the time of dense zooplankton blooms — clusters of microscopic animals feeding on plant matter generated during the spring. Copepods are particularly abundant and serve as nourishment for small shrimp, fish and the myriad other animals of the estuarine world.

But if summer is a time of youth, it is also still a time of birth for many marsh residents. Late-arriving migrant birds, such as the tern, will set up housekeeping in isolated areas not already occupied by other species.

In brackish water, killifish and mummichogs begin their breeding behavior, and their color changes as they prepare for the next generation. One of the more unusual of these small marsh fish is the stickleback, so-called because of the spines just forward of its soft dorsal fin. The American, or fourspine, stickleback *(Apeltes quadracus)* is the most common species along our Atlantic coast. During breeding time, usually in the summer, the male gathers plant debris and constructs a tunnel-shaped nest held together by mucus secreted from his kidneys. His usual grayish color will then change to courting shades of pink and orange to entice a willing female into his nest, which is securely attached to the base of some marine algae. After a few gentle prods on her tail by the male, the female will shed the eggs within the nest. She then swims away, and the male enters the nest to fertilize the eggs. This casanova of the salt-marsh world is not through, however — he will immediately lead another female to his nest. The procedure is repeated any number of times until the nest is full. The male now stands guard, defending the developing brood against all comers until the fry leave to begin their independent existence.

Close by, also going through its mating ritual, is the horseshoe crab *(Limulus polyphemus)*. This denizen of deeper water migrates to warm, shallow waters during June. Resembling a Sherman tank crossing the Sahara, this grotesque but harmless relative of the spider is often seen plowing along the bottom, literally pushing the sand aside as it scavenges for tiny crustaceans and mollusks. Limulus seems to have reached the end of an evolutionary trail; it has remained unchanged over millions of years. The male, smaller than the female, its front appendages modified into claspers, attaches itself to the back end of the female. During a moon tide, the couple crawls up to the high

reaches of the beach. The female scoops out a hollow and lays her eggs, which are immediately fertilized by the male. At the next moon tide, those eggs that have not been destroyed or eaten by the ever-present gulls will be set free into the water, where the larvae will undergo several molts, emerging each time more like a miniature adult. It will be another eight to ten years before these youngsters return to the beaches.

When not mating, the horseshoe crab is often seen enjoying the warm sun leisurely floating on its back, keeping that position in the water by slow movements of its book-like gills. Its hard-shell carapace seems to offer excellent protection, but when flipped on its back in the sand, a favorite trick employed by gulls, the creature is completely defenseless. Once the gills dry out, the animal dies, and its soft undersides make excellent protein for scavengers.

Plants as well as animals are involved in the process of reproduction, some with floral displays that are not always evident. The spartina grasses and spike grass have small, inconspicuous flowers, and eelgrass *(Zostera marina)*, an important flowering species, is completely submerged under the estuarine waters. The common name of this last plant is derived from the fact that its three-to-four-foot-long green blades resemble the size and shape of an adult eel. A pioneer in the formation of the salt marsh, eelgrass was instrumental in stabilizing the mudflats, its roots trapping the sediments and its fronds slowing the current enough to allow particulate matter to settle out of suspension.

Zostera marina has a wide range, inhabiting Atlantic and Pacific coastal areas of the United States, Asia and Europe, growing at depths of from three to thirty feet, depending upon the turbidity of the waters. It is not a grass, in spite of its appearance, but rather a submerged flowering plant, a member of the pond-weed family *Zosteraceae*. During the summer, when the water temperature has reached a critical level, the well-concealed flower is produced within the leaf blade, which then splits to allow pollination by water currents carrying the thread-like pollen to the female flower. Perhaps because of the uncertainty of such a mode of transfer, nature has provided a second method of propagation — by perennial rhizomes, or underground stems.

Around 1931, some organism, now suspected to have been the plant fungus *Labyrinthes*, invaded the eelgrass world along the North Atlantic coast, causing the leaves to develop black spots and both leaves and rhizomes to rot and die. Within three years the disease had spread to the west coast of the United States and to Europe and Asia, destroying about ninety per cent of the world's *Zostera*. Areas which formerly had abundant growth were no longer protected from the fury of the sea. Animals dependent upon eelgrass for protection, food or a natural habitat were now thrust into a strange new environment where chances for survival were considerably less.

In the course of evolution, the more specialized an organism becomes, the smaller its chances of survival. A case in point is the relationship between the koala bear and its only food source, eucalyptus leaves. Should the eucalyptus species develop a disease and die, the koala bear would probably become extinct. Such was the relationship between eelgrass and the American brant *(Branta bernicla)*. This small, black-necked goose relied almost exclusively on eelgrass for its nourishment and when the disease struck experienced a starvation diet which drastically reduced its numbers.

Eelgrass also serves as a substrate for young scallops. During June and July, as you wade through eelgrass or row a boat over it, you will see hundreds of tiny scallops attached to the blades a foot or more above the bottom. This is probably an adaptive measure to protect the delicate scallop from its natural enemies, who are continually roaming the bottom, and also to insure that young scallops will not suffocate in the mud. With the disappearance of the eelgrass scallops had no way of avoiding their enemies, and these shellfish declined in numbers, as did many other organisms — mostly microscopic zooplankton that depended upon the decayed products of these plants for their energy needs.

Eelgrass had a number of economic uses. Among these were as fertilizer, fuel, garden mulch and packing filler for fragile articles. In home construction, it was used for insulation and soundproofing. In some areas it is still harvested as a fodder for cattle. For ten long years the disease took its toll while industries dependent upon the grass went out of existence or changed to other forms of commerce. Fortunately, however, along the coastal regions of North America, Europe and Asia, where rivers empty into bays and dilute the saline seawater, the eelgrass was not affected, and from these plants have spread new strains to populate the waters once again.

Cod, herring and mackerel spend their earliest days in and

around the estuaries, taking advantage of the food coming off the marsh. So, too, do young bluefish, striped bass and the Atlantic croaker, which mumbles to himself as he swims along. The brood-carrying northern pipefish hides among the eelgrass, its upright, needle-like body perfectly blending with the swaying green blades.

All these fish and more make excellent meals for the terns, the gulls and the wading herons with their spear-like bills and long legs. The American and red-breasted mergansers are busy floating about near shore and diving for their diet of fish and small crustaceans. Summer on the marsh belongs to the birds. Grackles will come down to the wrack line — the high-water mark — to forage; the sandpiper is seen running parallel to the waterline, hardly getting its feet wet as it feeds on small isopods. Mallards join the mergansers in the water, but these ducks dive for plants, not animals.

The air is alive with swallows, willets, rails and red-winged blackbirds. Even a snowy-white American egret will be seen, although it is more common on the southern marshes, as is the American bittern, that master of camouflage, which is sometimes seen in northern marshes. When approached, it will stretch itself out to its full height and point its bill straight up in the air. The brownish and white striped feathers blend effectively against a background of water reeds, and if a wind is blowing the bird will sway with the oscillations of the grasses.

The two dominant mammals of the marsh, the raccoon and the muskrat, are seldom seen. Both are nocturnal and prefer to stay under cover, resting during the warm summer days. The muskrat, a relative of the beaver, is more aquatic than terrestrial. Rather clumsy on land, it is an excellent swimmer and prefers the marshy environment where it builds its lodges. Its diet of marsh-plant roots may be varied with mussels, clams, insects and fish. During a warm summer evening, another nocturnal visitor, a stray mink, will enter the marsh in search of insects and fish.

The most common mollusk of the eelgrass world is the scallop *(Pecten irradians)*. Its reproduction occurs during the summer, and after a period as a free-floating larval form, the scallop will attach itself to the eelgrass. Adult scallops possess two unequally curved shells, and lie with the more deeply curved one on the bottom. Algae and tube worms often attach themselves to the top shell and provide a degree of camouflage. When resting, the scallop has its shells agape, displaying two rows of beautiful deep-blue eyes. The scallop has developed two modes of swimming — both employing the principle of jet propulsion. By rapidly opening and closing its shells with its large round adductor muscle, it can direct water away from the hinge and move backwards. This is an escape mechanism especially necessary when the predator moon snail *(Lunatia heros)* or the starfish *(Asterias forbesi)* wanders by. For leisurely swimming, water is directed out the corners of the hinge to produce a forward motion. Groups of scallops are often seen swimming on the surface, each resembling a pair of dentures taking rapid bites as it migrates through the water.

By its nature, a salt marsh is relatively flat. The effect of runoff is minimized by its small slope and abundant grasses. Its peculiar character encourages certain communities of plants and animals. Likewise the terrestrial zone above the marsh has its special characteristics. Never experiencing the twice-daily flooding of the marsh, this zone favors such plants as the black, red and scrub oak, pitch pine, beach plum and bayberry.

Between the marsh and the terrestrial environment is a transitional zone that ecologists call an ecotone. This area supports a somewhat different kind of fauna and flora, and in many cases more species and a denser population, than either of the adjoining zones. Most of the flowering plants of the summer marsh are found here.

The earliest marsh rush to mature is the black grass *(Juncus Gerardi)*. Its brownish-black fruit matures in June, giving a dark periphery to the borders of the marsh during the summer and remaining quite conspicuous well into October. The prostrate or upright stems of the sand spurrey *(Spergularia marina)*, with their fleshy green linear leaves, give rise to small pink flowers. Bright yellow flowers adorn the silverweed *(Potentilla anserina)*, whose deeply toothed leaves, silvery-white on the underside with a deep green top, are as attractive as its blossoms. The white, lavender or pink bell-shaped flower of the sea milkwort *(Glaux maritima)* contrasts sharply with the brown spikelets of the early blooming chairmaker's rush *(Scirpus americanus)*.

The parade of colors continues with the small white flowers of the perennial late seaside plantain *(Plantago oliganthos)*, the pale green of sea blite *(Suaeda maritima)*, the golden lemon-yellow of the slender-leaved goldenrod *(Solidago tenuifolia)*, the pink and rose-purple of seaside gerardia *(Gerardia maritima)* and the white or pink of seabeach knotweed *(Polygonum glaucum)* growing flat on the ground. In small depressions where evaporation may increase salinity is the most beautiful plant of the marsh — the sea lavender *(Limonium carolinianum)*. Its two-foot-high, woody, highly branched stem is adorned with lovely tiny lavender blossoms rising from a rosette of leathery green leaves. A conspicuous plant of the summer marsh is the swamp rose mallow *(Hibiscus palustris)*. Viewed from the uplands, this transitional-zone flower, with its three- to four-inch-diameter blossom of pink or cream, stands out like a jeweled garnet against a distant green carpet.

During August the halberd-leaved orach *(Atriplex patula* var. *hastata)* with its green triangular-shaped leaves is topped by tiny green flowers. Coast blite *(Chenopodium rubrum)* with its small clusters of red flowers gives a delightful contrast to the green of the marsh grasses. These flowers will remain until the first frost, turning a brilliant red in the fall. An especially easy flower to identify is the salt-marsh fleabane *(Pluchea purpurascens* var. *succulenta)*. Its stem and leaves are both very thick, and the pink or purple flower forms flat-topped clusters.

Sedges and reeds push their roots into the soft mud; their tall, flexible strands sway gently in the breeze. Muskrats prowl around and gnaw on the roots of the cat-tails, and ducks come to nest in dense clusters of these brackish-water plants. In the transitional zone we see more terrestrial animals, such as snakes, frogs and even an occasional nocturnal weasel hunting for mice among the cat-tails.

One of the world's most beautiful reeds inhabits this brackish-water environment. The giant common reed *Phragmites communis* forms in tight homogeneous groves six or more feet high. During late September and into autumn, it is at its most spectacular, with plumes of brownish red swaying in the wind.

Poison ivy is usually associated with a drier terrestrial habitat, but often this rugged plant with its shiny, deep green leaves will grow along marsh borders. Its leaves turn a beautiful bright red in the fall, belying its obnoxious characteristics.

Three species of *Salicornia* inhabit the marsh proper. Woody glasswort *(Salicornia virginica)* is a perennial, while dwarf glasswort *(S. Bigelovii)* and samphire *(S. europaea)* are annuals. *Salicornia virginica* has a woody center and forms sizable mats on the marsh floor. Growing from a creeping main stem, its upright, unbranched portion is a translucent green, turning to gray in the autumn. The annual species have several common names indicative of their wide range. They have been called samphire, glasswort, marsh pickle, saltwort and chickentoes. Annuals have swollen branched succulent stems which were used by early colonists in salads, raw or often pickled. All species have tiny flowers embedded in the hollows of the upper joints of the spikes. The annuals add a late touch of beauty to the marsh when their green stems turn to various hues of red and orange in the fall.

It may be said that the spartina grasses are what the salt marsh is all about. All other plants that inhabit the marsh are insignificant compared to the importance and density of the salt-water cord and salt-meadow grasses, whose sheer volume provides nearly all necessary nutrients and protection for the marsh inhabitants, while their perennial underground stems hold the marsh together. Both species, *alterniflora* and *patens*, are perennial grasses. Toward the end of summer, the exposed blades push their seed-laden heads above the normal level of the grass, where the wind can disperse the seed in and around the marsh. Many fall on hostile ground, to be eaten or blown into the sea where they become nutrient for fish and ducks. Even for the seeds that germinate, competition from established perennials, especially for light, will eliminate most of them. Nonetheless, spartina grass survives and spreads.

Northern marshes lack any trees comparable to the magnificent mangroves of the South, a circumstance due almost entirely to the climate. The cold winters of the North can cause sea water to freeze into ice cakes that are pushed across the marsh, shearing off all vegetation. A woody-stemmed tree would have a most difficult time becoming established. There is, however, a sizable shrub growing to a height of nine feet that is found on the borders of all the marshes along the entire coast. This is the groundsel tree, or sea myrtle *(Baccharis halimifolia)* — a dioecious shrub with pistillate (female) and staminate (male) blossoms on separate plants. The pistillate flower has white or yellow blossoms from August through October.

All is not peace, quiet and beauty in the salt marsh, for summer is the season of the greenhead flies and mosquitoes. The large, fleshy-lobed white maggots of the greenhead flies *(Tabanus)* have pupated and now emerge as adults. The common marsh mosquito *(Aedes sollicitans)* lays its eggs on the wet muddy ground in the upland, where rain or a high tide will form the puddles necessary for their hatching. Man has fought a long battle with the distasteful and sometimes deadly mosquito. Control measures have included spreading oil upon marsh waters to clog the breathing tubes of the larvae (wigglers). Drainage ditches have been cut to eliminate standing bodies of water, and spraying with various chemicals has been tried. All these methods had some degree of success in eliminating the mosquito, but at the same time they caused irreparable harm to the fauna and flora of the marsh.

One method used on selected marshes where the water level can be controlled is to flood the entire area to a level higher than normal. The eggs, larvae or pupae are thereby set adrift and become more available to the insect-eating fish and birds.

High tide during the summer is feeding time for most insect-eating birds. Those flying insects that are in the transi-

tional stage between nymphs and adults still cannot fly, and as the tide floods, most of these air-breathers must escape the rising waters by crawling up the stalks of marsh plants. There they are easy pickings for gulls, terns, wrens and swallows. The salt-marsh snail *(Melampus)*, is also eaten by birds, for this snail's shell can be used for grinding food in the birds' crops.

In the heat of the summer, song birds often retire to nearby upland trees to escape the penetrating rays of the sun. Their departure does not necessarily put a stop to the music, however, for this is the time when the marsh musicians, the grasshoppers and crickets, tune up their instruments. By rubbing parts of his body together (stridulation), the male of the species, usually, emits sound, but he can play only when he is on the ground, not having perfected his talent while airborne.

Marsh waters are not without their share of aristocracy. Both the horseshoe crab and blue crab possess blue blood, due to the presence in it of copper. The substance responsible for carrying oxygen to the cells of the body is the molecule hemoglobin. In higher animals, the hemoglobin contains iron, giving the blood a red color. When copper is substituted for the iron, as in the blue crab and horseshoe crab, the blood takes on a bluish tinge.

The blue crab *(Callinectes sapidus)* is sometimes found in deep water, but is far more frequently seen in brackish or nearly fresh estuaries. It is the largest commercially grown crab on the Atlantic coast, often measuring six inches or more across its shell. Along with the lobster, it is one of our most important seafood products.

Callinectes is a powerful swimmer, because its last pair of appendages has been modified into paddles. Sharp, knife-like claws make this decapod a formidable adversary. As with all members of the arthropod group, the exoskeleton of the blue crab must be shed periodically to allow growth to continue. A crab without its protective armor is quite vulnerable to its natural enemies and will usually hide when it is molting. Immediately after shedding its outer skeleton, *Callinectes* is knows as a "soft shell," the condition in which it is most highly prized, for it can then be cooked and eaten in its entirety.

The most celebrated and numerous animal on the marsh, sometimes numbering more than a million per acre, is the fiddler crab. Actually, there are three species of fiddlers that live here: *Uca pugnax*, *U. pugilator* and *U. minax*, the first two, somewhat smaller than the last, being the most common. Young fiddlers of both sexes have pairs of small claws. The female's remain the same throughout life, but the right claw of the male, the fiddle, continues to grow until it is a much enlarged anomaly which seems too clumsy for this small, one-inch crab.

Fiddlers live in tunnels that they have constructed on the banks of marsh-creeks. These tunnels may extend obliquely down as much as three feet, ending in a horizontal chamber deep enough so that the rising tide can moisten its walls. These fiddler species have evolved into a nearly terrestrial form, with much reduced gills and a highly vascularized branchial chamber which needs only to be damp for the crab to breathe, an adaptation which permits this non-swimming creature to remain out of water for a month or more at a time.

Mating occurs during the summer. The male will take up a post just outside his tunnel, stretch himself to his full height by standing on tiptoe, and project his periscopic eye even higher to watch for the mate of his choice. The female will crawl by in alluring fashion, setting up a strange behavior pattern in the male. He begins to do deep-knee bends, swinging his enormous claw in his own special way. If the female is impressed, she will accompany him to his tunnel where mating will occur. The female will lay her eggs and attach them to her abdomen. Periodically she can be seen scurrying to the edge of the water to wash them. When ready, the eggs will be released into the water and carried off by

A wonderful weekend
with wonderful people!
Rebecca Buchthel
August, 1985

tides and currents to develop into a larval stage called a zoea, which, after several molts, resembles the adult. Most of the eggs are eaten by fish or birds, but enough survive for a new beginning.

The fiddler will only be seen during an ebbing tide. Huge numbers tramp through the spartina grasses or along the mud banks, picking up plant and animal detritus lying on the exposed mud floor.

Biological rhythms are a much-studied phenomenon, especially in the fiddler crab, for it seems this fellow possesses not one, but two, internal clocks — a lunar cycle which correlates the activity of the crab with the tides, and a solar cycle which initiates color changes. Fiddlers are a dark, blackish-brown during daylight hours, but gradually turn a light gray in the evening.

Sometimes, the fiddle claw seems to be on the wrong side; while most are right-handed fiddlers, some are left-handed. If the male should lose his large claw in an encounter with a gull or his bigger neighbor, the purple marsh crab *(Sesarum cinereum)*, the left claw will hypertrophy until it is the size of the original fiddle; the severed claw will be replaced by one of a normal size. Thus *Uca* has the capacity to become an ambidextrous fiddler.

So the economy of the marsh continues, with plants providing nutrient for the larger herbivores while the microscopic vegetation of the creeks, the phytoplankton, contributes to the food chain of the sea. Energy passes from producer to consumer, from herbivore to carnivore, each a vital link in a never-ending chain of events in which every plant and animal plays its appointed role.

But now the sun's rays do not feel as warm during the day and there is a touch of chill in the night air. Blossoms have accomplished their purpose and the the slow process of senescence sets in. Though still beautiful, the radiance of the colored petals gradually diminishes.

Rain comes more frequently; birds sense a difference and become fidgety. The fall of the leaf heralds harvest time.

Autumn
The Time of Fulfillment

The long, hot days of July and August have heated the coastal waters to a comfortable temperature. The shallow creeks, inlets and bays have served their nursery function, providing protection and food for the young marine animals during their early development.

But now shortening days mean fewer hours of warming sunlight, and the summer's heat is slowly dissipated into the atmosphere. As the surface of the sea cools, it becomes slightly heavier than the layers of water below and begins to sink. The warmer layers near the bottom are pushed up, carrying with them the detritus that has accumulated during the previous months. These added nutrients, particularly the nitrates and phosphates, contribute to another phytoplankton bloom, although not nearly so dense as that of the spring. With an increase in food supply, there is a corresponding rise in the number of animals feeding in the marsh waters.

Small fish and crustaceans leave the shallows and head for deeper water; some migrate further south where winters are not as severe. In the New England area, summer flounder (*Paralichthys dentatus*) will leave protected inland waters and return to their winter home at the edge of the continental shelf, where there is a much narrower range of temperature. The winter flounder (*Pseudopleuronectes americanus*), a hardier breed, come in from the shelf area where they have spent the summer and enter the shallow bays and estuaries where they will remain until the spring.

Flounder are unusual in their development. They seem to be flattened from top to bottom instead of the usual side-to-side. Actually, when flounder, or flatfish as they are also called, are very young, one eye starts to migrate toward the other — resulting in both ending up on the same side of the body. At the same time, the side missing the eye takes on a whitish color and assumes the ventral (bottom) position. The top side, containing both eyes, develops dark pigment cells called chromatophores, which are useful as camouflage. This coloration pattern, light on the bottom and dark on the top, is known as countershading and is usual in most fish. With its mouth opening from left to right and its dorsal and ventral fins in a horizontal plane, this anatomically mixed-up fish is destined forever to swim the side stroke close to the bottom, feeding on small crustaceans, mollusks and seaworms.

As a general rule, fish are a migratory lot, being constantly on the move in search of food and influenced by changing water temperatures. Along with the summer flounder, other species leave for the continental shelf as the inshore waters cool. The scup, hake and fluke move out of marsh creeks and estuaries for the less variable temperatures of the deep. Bass and menhaden accompany them, but will not travel as far offshore. Pelagic or ocean fish, like tuna and bluefish, will be somewhat regulated in their migration by seasonal changes. They travel north with the spring, coming inshore to the spawning area or where food is plentiful, and head south in the fall, feeding near the mouths of large estuaries on schools of departing young fish.

Some of the smaller creek fish remain within the marsh waters all winter. The mummichog, banded killifish and minnow all are year-round residents. When the cooling water slows their swimming agility, they are easy targets for the larger fish or the birds that prey on them. Toward the end of autumn, most of these small marsh fish have dug into the upper layers of mud in the creeks, to remain in a state of stupor until winter passes.

The period encompassing the end of summer and the first weeks of autumn is breeding time for the marsh insects. The most obnoxious pest in this group is the mosquito (*Aedes sollicitans*). The primary adult role of most insects is to procreate, and the mosquito's is no different. Females will lay their eggs in and around the marsh where the tide or the rain has created a puddle. In a few days, the eggs hatch into larvae, called wigglers, that hang head downward in the water and breathe by means of a tube projecting to the water's surface. These wigglers develop into pupae within a week and emerge from their watery environment as adults within two or three days after that. The whole process of metamorphosis from egg to adult takes about two weeks, depending upon the temperature. The adults will mate later in the autumn, and the eggs will remain dormant until the first of the spring rains starts the cycle again. Of course, not all eggs will hatch; some will never survive through the winter. Some will be eaten by birds, while still others will be washed into tidal creeks by storms and there be eaten by fish. Enough survive, however, to begin mosquito life again in the spring.

Grasshoppers, crickets, greenhead flies and midges — in fact most insects — will survive through the winter in one of the stages of metamorphosis. Eggs, larvae and pupae have a remarkable ability to sustain themselves in harsh environments. Eggs and pupae will remain dormant for months, while larval forms will crawl down into the soft marsh peat where temperatures are less severe.

Labor Day marks the unofficial end of summer, although the autumnal equinox is still weeks away. Vacationers head for home, students dust off their books, and the small tourist shops and motels begin closing, one by one, leaving the coastal regions to the year-round inhabitants.

Though many warm and beautiful days remain, somehow the migrant birds sense a change in the shortening days. Those that have great distances to go have spent the past weeks building up a stored fat supply to sustain them during the long flight ahead. Not all birds migrate, and there are always a few individuals from the migratory species that remain behind for one reason or another. Food, the constant source of energy all living creatures must have, is now in shortening supply, and this fact must be a primary impetus directing some birds southward to places where winter dormancy is less pronounced.

Most of the birds that migrate southward are the seed- or

insect-eaters, birds of prey and the water birds. The first trickle of migration begins in late summer or early fall, as the white-breasted tree swallows leave for their winter quarters along the coast from North Carolina to Florida. A few swallows may prefer to remain behind and winter in the northern cat-tail and *Phragmites* marshlands.

The golden plover (*Pluvialis dominica*) is seen on the Atlantic coast only in autumn. In the spring, it migrates northward through the Mississippi valley to the Arctic where it breeds, while its autumn migration takes it down the Atlantic coastal flyway as far as North Carolina. At this jumping-off spot, the plover begins a long ocean flight to South America, where it may winter as far south as Argentina. The Hudsonian curlew (*Numenius phaeopus hudsonicus*) follows the plover south from its breeding ground in the Arctic to South America as well.

As a general rule, the wading birds — herons, rails, oyster

catchers, bitterns, egrets and sandpipers — travel in a leisurely fashion down to more southerly marshes of the United States, where the marine life on which they feed is more abundant.

All herons are great fisherman — wading out into the marsh creeks to a depth appropriate to the length of their legs and waiting patiently for their catch. The technique of the green heron (*Butorides virescens*) is worth recounting. This small heron will drop a piece of food from its bill upstream and then crouch low on the bank below to avoid casting its shadow on the water. Keeping a wary eye on the bait as it floats by, the heron waits silently, often repeating its "cast" several times. At the first sign of a nibble, the bird plunges its head into the water and invariably comes up with a fish. This process is repeated again and again until the heron's appetite is satisfied.

Birds of prey, especially the hawk, head south as soon as their main food supply, small rodents, becomes scarce. Years ago, it was a common sight to see a hundred or more hawks gathered at the head of the large estuaries as they made their fall journey. But of late, hunters have taken their toll of this valuable species and only a few are left to grace the heavens as they sail effortlessly aloft.

The shedding of seeds by the marsh plants is a sign to the seed-eating birds to begin their saltatory pattern of hop-skipping southward from marsh to marsh. A few northern seed-eaters like the finches and sparrows remain to eke out a meager existence until the spring. This same unhurried migration is practiced by most insect eaters, although the eggs, larvae or pupae deposited in marsh mud or between cracks in the bark of trees will provide those who stay behind with sustenance over the winter.

Swimming coots and grebes love warm water and leave at the first signs of a chill, while the black duck, the most common duck of the marshes, and the blue-winged teal brave the chilly waters and stay well into winter. They will remain in the North throughout the year as long as there is open water. Red-breasted mergansers, pintails and some bitterns are reluctant to leave and can often be seen in winter around the open marsh-creeks.

Along the entire east coast, the bird most commonly seen at the shore is the herring gull (*Larus argentatus*). This scavenger has a wide range — breeding on the beach and near shore islands from New Jersey to the Arctic and wintering everywhere on the Atlantic coast. The downy, grayish-brown chicks peck out of their olive-speckled eggs laid by the female during the early summer. Their first plumage is a dirty brown, which lightens in color with each molt. After three years, they are adult birds, with gray mantles, black wing-tips and pale, flesh-colored legs.

An independent cuss, the herring gull is intelligent and alert. It will often roam the beaches in the evening to prey on the weaker petrels or other small birds as they come in to land for rest or to feed. Eating the eggs or chicks of other birds is a not-uncommon practice of the herring gull. Fishermen report seeing gulls actually knocking weaker birds out of flight over the ocean, causing them to drown and become a feast for the aggressor. Gulls do not migrate as a group, and as long as food is available they will stay all winter. They divide their time between the coastal waters and the open dumps that are so common in small towns. Where the herring gull goes, there too goes his sidekick, the black-backed gull (*Larus marinus*), who seems content to be a follower. A trip to a garbage dump near the coast can almost always provide the bird watcher with the sight of hundreds of herring gulls all standing uniformly facing the wind, quite oblivious to the approach of automobile or human.

New Englanders associate autumn with the silent explosion of colored leaves. At no other time of the year does nature display her brilliance so vividly. It would seem that the bright yellows of the birch and poplar, the red hues of the dogwood, the tans of the white oak, the purple of the ash and the brilliant reds and oranges of the sugar maples should convince even the most inflexible agnostic that this variegation of foliage is not a mere chance event.

The cooling temperatures of autumn seem not to be the controlling factor over the parade of color; the event can be predicted with reasonable accuracy regardless of the weather. It seems reasonable to assume, with much evidence to support the assumption, that the activities of most plants and animals are somehow fundamentally linked to the changing length of day and night.

Although not nearly so splashy as tree foliage, the marsh plants have their own special autumn beauty. Flat-topped clusters of pink or purple fleabane are short-lived and go soon after summer's end, as does the creamy-white flower of ladies' tresses (*Spiranthes cernua*), but the tiny green blossoms of the halberd-leaved orach will remain throughout October. Sea lavender, its woody branched stem adorned with lavender or light purple flowers, adds a delicate touch unsurpassed in other marsh plants.

The perennial woody glasswort (*Salicornia virginica*) will turn a dull gray, but the greens of its annual cousins S. *Bigelovii* and S. *europaea* become hues of reds and oranges, giving an unexpected brilliance to the marsh floor. The small cluster of coast blite flowers (*Chenopodium rubrum*) changes to a vermilion that will persist until the first frost.

On the borders of the marsh, black grass (*Juncus Gerardi*), turned quite gray by now, stands out like a host of dark sentinels saying, "from here to the sea is the domain of the marsh." On the marsh floor, the grasses gradually lose their chlorophyll and hues of lighter greens and yellows gradually invade the green blades. The yellow-to-rust spikelets of the sedge (*Cyperus*) and the brown-purple of the salt-reed grass (*Spartina cynosuroides*) brighten the marsh well into November in a mild winter. Canary-yellow flowers of the slender-leaved goldenrod and the

brilliant scarlet leaves of the poison ivy present a vivid contrast to the dull browns of the scrub oaks in the uplands.

Most conspicuous of all the grasses in the brackish parts of the marsh is the tall, feathery-plumed reed, *Phragmites communis*. The plumes, which persist well into winter, make *Phragmites* the most distinguished of all marsh plants, especially during the latter part of autumn and early winter, when most other plants are dormant.

Soon after the marsh grasses have set their seed, growth slows down and eventually stops. Just as the leaf of the deciduous tree weakens at its petiole (leaf stem), so does *Spartina patens* weaken at its base. Cold biting winds, whistling in from offshore, push against the salt hay, causing it to topple like so many rows of toy soldiers. As autumn wears on, the beautifully manicured marsh-grass lawn of the summer becomes a tousled array of swirls — ready now to be harvested.

Long before our present grasslands were established, seacoast farmers hand-cut the spartina grass for use as animal fodder. Later, horses were used to pull a cutter over the marsh. Special shoes, resembling wooden snowshoes, were fitted to the horses' hoofs to prevent them from sinking into the soft peat base. As civilization moved westward and industry replaced agriculture on the eastern seaboard, the salt marsh played a role of declining utility, though as late as the 1930's some sea farmers were still harvesting the marsh hay.

Working between the ever-present tides, the hay was cut and piled on racks to dry. These racks, called staddles, consisted of a wooden or stone framework, circular in shape and fifteen to twenty feet in diameter, elevated on legs above the high-tide mark. Attached pulley systems aided the farmer in lifting the heavy grass. Like an ocean liner whose hawsers are equipped with rat guards, these staddles stood like schooners on the marsh, their supporting legs also fitted with horizontal metal discs to prevent the entry of small rodents into the hay. Skeletal remains of abandoned staddles can be seen today on some of the extensive *Spartina patens* marshes between New England and North Carolina.

Farming salt-meadow hay is not altogether a lost art. In isolated areas men still harvest the grass. Because it is weed-free, the hay is useful as a packing material and as a garden mulch. Today a mechanized industry exists to harvest about ten thousand acres of marsh on the west side of Cape May in southern New Jersey. Dikes have been built at the seaward edge of the marsh with sluice gates to regulate the flow and ebb of the sea. Tractors and balers have replaced the farmer and his horse, causing a little more nostalgic Americana to vanish from the scene.

As autumn wears on, other marsh residents leave for a more hospitable environs. The blue-blooded aristocrats, the horseshoe crab and the blue crab, are not particularly fond of cold water and leave soon after the majority of fish have departed. Little by little, the marsh is being depleted of all except her most hardy tenants.

From late spring until the middle of autumn, the fiddler crabs have been making their twice-daily scavenger missions around the marsh, descending into their underground tunnels as the tide rises. Fiddlers are sun-worshippers, and when the temperature dips to the sixties you will have seen the last of them. Within the safety of their homes, the fiddlers' metabolism slows and they go into a winter stupor, not feeding again until the following spring.

Not all animals' metabolism slows down in colder weather, however. Experiments have shown that the common mole crab *(Emertia talpoida)* has a metabolic rate at 37°F. four times as great as in the summer at 75°F. Thus its activity remains high and growth continues during the winter.

This peculiar crab does not have the flattened-out body of its normal cousins but rather, when its last abdominal segment (telson) is tucked under its body, presents the general shape of a football. Mole is a well-deserved name for this crab, which migrates up and down the beach with the tides, burrowing just below the surface of the sand. The digging is correlated with its peculiar manner of feeding. As the nutrient-laden waves roll up the beach, the mole crab will turn to face the ocean and project its pair of feathery feeding antennae. As the wave slides back down the beach, microscopic food particles cling to the outstretched antennae which then direct them into the crab's mouth. Unless dislodged by heavy surf and cast up high on the beach where scavengers may eat it, or scratched out of its sandy burrow by any of the shore birds, the mole crab spends its entire life span of just over one year scurrying up and down beaches feeding on the outgoing waves.

Shellfish, as a general rule, do not migrate, although we have seen that the scallop can propel itself through the water. Clams of all types can burrow into the sand or mud to obtain some degree of protection. Others, like the oyster and the mussel, have limited or no movement. Despite its inability to escape predators, such a mollusk would seem to be comfortably secure within its tight thick shell. Two of the most voracious predators, however, the moon snail *(Lunatia heros)* and the sand-collar snail *(Polinices duplicatus)*, are a continual threat to mollusk security as they roam the bottom or burrow deep within the sand. The larger, *L. heros,* can extend its massive foot eight or ten inches, to engulf such prey easily. Its radula, a scraping tongue, makes a small hole on the valve (shell) of its victim. Then a small amount of acid drips from a special gland in the snail's foot and eats away the valve, creating a perfectly round aperture though which the soft flesh of the shellfish is sucked out. The range of these two gastropods rarely overlaps. The smaller sand-collar snail is content to remain in shallow waters, leaving the offshore territory to its larger counterpart. Predation by these two carnivorous snails goes on throughout the year.

Kathy Simmons
"Life is there, just
let it free!"
8/11/85

As November ploughs its chilly days into the cold of December, the machinery of the northern marsh slows to an almost dormant state. The animals meet the temperature problem in a number of ways, though in general we can say that they either adjust to it or migrate. Most resident birds that remain seek shelter in the upland woods, as does the white-tailed deer. Small mammals such as voles, rats and chipmunks begin their winter sleep. Raccoons crawl into their nests for varying periods of sleep during which their metabolic processes slow down, though they are not true hibernators. Adult insects have succumbed with the first frost, and their offspring are safely tucked away for the winter. Most fish have gone to warmer waters, leaving the inlets and bays to the winter flounder and long-horned sculpin.

As winter settles in, the guardianship of the marsh is left to the herring gull, who will keep a lonely vigil over his domain until spring once more creeps back from the South.

Winter
The Time of Rest

Winter on the northern marshes is a time of leanness. Even though algae within the creeks continue to carry on photosynthesis, the food supply for the marsh animals consists mainly of summer's leftovers, which decrease with each passing day. The amount of radiant energy reaching the marsh diminishes. Darkness comes early and stays late.

But life goes on beneath the cold mantle of winter. Though the green, well-manicured fields of spartina grass have become acres of faded yellow, brown and straw-colored stubble, they still supply a major part of the nutrient of the marsh. Bacterial action decomposes the spartina and the detritus becomes part of the rich upper layers of peat. Some of the organic matter washes into the tidal creeks and out to the bays, making the waters more fertile. Part of this organic nutrient finds its way down to the bottom layers of the water and will contribute to the plankton bloom following next year's spring overturn.

Specially adapted to carrying on photosynthesis during the winter, the mud algae embedded along the creeks continue their food-making activities when the sun warms the exposed mud at low tide. Winter is also a time when the coastal waters are the clearest and the photic zone (the depth to which sunlight can penetrate) is the deepest — thus the phytoplankton are producing food and the zooplankton forms grow even in the coldest months. Within marsh creeks a few hardy individual fish still swim, but the numbing cold has made their movements labored and sluggish. Fish have a permanent anti-freeze in their blood, but it is only effective down to certain temperature levels. Once the water approaches its freezing point, most of the small marsh fish, such as mummichogs, killifish and minnows, have dug into the bottom mud. Because of the variations that exist among all species, a few still swim — easy pickings for hungry water-birds and gulls. The pelagic species that have come in to shore for the winter remain relatively inactive, especially during the coldest weeks of winter.

Other than the few evergreen pines and cedars in the uplands, the only green to be seen throughout the winter around the marsh is that of the submerged eelgrass *(Zostera marina).* This flowering plant's peculiar growth pattern is regulated by the temperature of the water. Growth tissue remains dormant whenever the water temperature is below 50°F. At this critical point, however, its seeds will germinate; at 59°F., the tiny flower blooms, and between 59 and 68°F., fertilization of the flower by thread-like pollen traveling through the water will take place. Above 68°F., reached during the summer in northern marshes, growth ceases until the water temperature has dropped below 50°F. and has begun to rise again the following year.

In the brackish areas of the upland marsh, the stately reed, *Phragmites communis,* remains standing in dense clusters. Its withered, feather-like plumes still wave atop its six-foot stems, only now the whole plant has taken on a straw-like color. Freezing winter rain will coat *Phragmites* with layers of ice that glisten in the low winter sun. In this condition, the reeds resemble fields of frozen stalagmites rising majestically from the marsh floor.

Snow presents no problem to the marsh animals. If anything, it acts as an insulator and holds in some of the heat that would otherwise radiate into the atmosphere. But snow, even in severe storms, does not usually stay around for long. The salt in the air and water soon melts even the most persistent patches.

Ice, on the other hand, is a serious problem, because animals that have dug beneath the frost-line within the marsh still require oxygen. An ice cover will cut off their supply of air, and should it persist for any length of time, many of these animals, especially the numerous marine worms that lie below the surface, will die. Fiddler crabs, however, will not be affected by an ice cover. Deep within the marsh, the rising tide keeps the walls of their tunnels moist enough to supply the oxygen they need.

Ice cakes that may form during a severe cold winter will be pushed atop the marsh on a high tide. The jostling of the heavy cakes grinds all the standing stubble to the level of the marsh, perhaps killing off a few plants, but in the balance of nature probably doing more good than harm, as added plant detritus increases the richness of the soil.

Animal activity has now slowed to a minimum. On the marsh floor, the ribbed mussel remains, anchored by its byssus threads, filter-feeding on the high tide. Cold water does not seem to affect the mollusks; in fact, experiments have shown that some can survive a period of actually being frozen.

Raccoons, besides undergoing varying periods of rest during the cold weather, usually mate in the winter. On mild evenings during January and February, the raccoon will often be seen roaming the marsh creeks searching for mussels, clams or the carcass of some less fortunate animal. Muskrats will feed all winter off the roots of brackish-water marsh plants, particularly cat-tails. But if the plants are sealed beneath snow and ice, the muskrat will not hesitate to dive into the frigid water to hunt for fish, clams or mussels. In the evening, the carnivorous mink will leave his den in nearby woods and prowl the marsh and shore looking for food. The largest mammal likely to be seen will be the white-tailed deer, who has momentarily left the safety of the woodlands to browse on the shrubs near shore.

Often during winter, northeast storms will whip in off the Atlantic, bringing with them several species of birds that normally remain well out to sea. At these times the visitor to the coast may get a glimpse of the alcids, the class of ocean birds closest to the penguins in this part of the world. Alcids somewhat resemble ducks, but have small stubby necks and narrow wings. Some species have their legs set so far back on their bodies that, standing, they are nearly erect, like a penguin.

Auks, puffins and murres, which make up this group of sea birds, spend nearly all their lives on the ocean off the eastern coast of northern Maine and Canada, coming inshore to nest on

high cliffs. In winter these alcids may be blown ashore as far south as New Jersey.

On land perhaps the most helpless member of this family is the dovekie *(Plautus alle)* — the smallest of the winter sea birds. This chubby, neckless seven-inch bird has the typical alcid coloration of the penguin: black on top with white undersides. Its wings are small and narrow, and its tiny webbed feet are set far back. The position of the feet makes walking a rather clumsy activity, to the degree that the dovekie is never able to get up enough ground speed to become airborne. To attain flight from the ground, the dovekie must launch itself from a high cliff. On the ocean, however, its tiny webbed feet act like an outboard motor, easily propelling it across the water and into the air.

Another bird that is often blown in is the black-legged kittiwake — an open-ocean gull slightly smaller than the herring

gull but having solid black wing-tips. Kittiwakes normally remain well out to sea during the winter, eating what fish are available and sleeping on the ocean. Their winter sojourns may take them as far south as the Grand Banks and George's Banks, where the prospects of catching fish are better than they are farther north.

Although herring gulls are the most numerous birds around the northern shores and marshes, there are a few others that remain all or most of the winter. The beautiful Canada goose *(Branta canadensis)* will winter along the entire coast. Geese are more terrestrial than ducks and are often seen feeding off the remains of the spartina grasses and other stubble close to shore. Brant *(Branta bernicla)* also winter along the coast as far south as the Carolinas. They are the least terrestrial of the geese and feed on water plants, especially eelgrass and sea lettuce.

The most common winter duck is the black duck *(Anas rubripes)*, a surface feeder and thus particularly at home in shallow marsh waters. It obtains food by tipping down rather than by diving. Surface feeders are powerful flyers and can spring from the water directly into flight without running to get up speed. Fair-weather surface feeders also include the mallards, pintails and teals.

Southern marshes present a sharp contrast to the "seasonal" marshes of the more northern coastal regions. In South Carolina, Georgia and Florida, the spartina grasses grow, to some extent, all year long. There is a short transitional period following the setting of their seeds, but new growth begins again during the winter. Algae will grow all year long in all marshes.

Grasshoppers, the mud crab sesarme, plant hoppers and chinch bugs will continue to eat or suck juices from the spartina, but the fiddler crabs prefer to sleep during the winter even as far south as Georgia.

Most of the water and shore birds that accepted northern

hospitality during warmer weather find winter sanctuaries in the South, where food is plentiful, temperatures are mild and the marshes are more extensive, providing less competition for nesting and more protection against intruders.

In general, then, life in the South goes on as usual, but at a slower pace.

In the North, life has come almost to a standstill; noises have subsided to the level of an occasional whisper. The few animals that show some activity venture out intermittently and then only when absolutely necessary to obtain food. Even then their catch is meager.

The world of the salt marsh awaits the spring.

"NO HELL NOR HEAVEN SHALL THAT SOUL SURPRISE
WHO LOVES THE RAIN AND LOVES HIS HOME
AND LOOKS AT LIFE WITH QUIET EYES"

DOT HANDE —

A Time for Understanding

Though each individual salt marsh is unique in the sense that it has its own set of peculiar characteristics and its own specific stresses and strains, all have general patterns in common.

The dominant plant of the marsh may differ depending upon the latitude, the lay of the land, the tidal action of the ocean and the runoff of fresh water, yet the food chain is always basically similar. Radiant energy is captured by the chlorophyll-laden plants and, through a series of complex chemical reactions, is locked up as stored chemical energy within a food molecule. The food is then passed through an interwoven food web to herbivore, carnivore and omnivore. Bacterial action will eventually decompose all the organic matter to form basic materials which are again taken up and recycled through a multitude of pathways, keeping the whole ecosystem in balance. Each animal and plant within the marsh-estuarine system has its own specific role in regular interaction with other organisms of the biotic community and physical environment in such a way that an essential harmony is maintained.

It can be said that the fauna and flora which inhabit the marsh-estuarine ecosystem, as in any other ecosystem, do so because they have adapted to the particular set of conditions that are present. For each environmental factor there is a range within maximum and minimum limits that the organism can tolerate. Within this range, life processes proceed favorably. If the limits of its tolerance are exceeded, the organism must leave or die.

During the past seventy years our coastal zone, including the salt marshes, has been continually altered by man, particularly by channel dredging in tidal estuaries; coastal mining and drilling; land development for homes, industries, marinas, parking lots, highways and recreational areas; and by the use of marshes for waste disposal. Estuarine waters have been rendered inhospitable to life by industrial wastes, sewage, thermal pollution, pesticides and, more recently, nuclear wastes. Each change within the ecosystem brings the resident organisms closer to the limit of their physiological tolerance. Natural processes also produce their share of pollution, but very seldom do these push the organisms to their limits. The real danger to the delicate wetlands stems from humanity's compulsive drive to "improve" and conquer nature and acquire its wealth.

In the name of improvement, man has often upset the balance of nature and created a host of new problems more serious than those he set out to solve. A classic example of this is the Aswan High Dam project in Egypt. The advantages of this monumental project were supposed to be the elimination of the annual flooding of the Nile River, the creation of increased hydroelectric power, and an increase in the number of acres of arable land with a subsequent growth in food production, all worthwhile and commendable aims. Since 1964 when the dam first went into operation, the rich, mineral- and silt-laden Nile has no longer flooded the land, thus fertilizing it naturally. Now, upwards of $100-million per year must be expended for artificial fertilizer. The same natural nutrients from the river formerly supplied food for the Mediterranean sardine, which supported a huge fishing industry. Without these nutrients, the food chain was broken, depriving an enormous fish population of its accustomed source of subsistence and causing the sardine catch to decline from some 20,000 tons annually in 1965 to its present annual level of less than 500 tons. In addition, other valuable marine species have disappeared — notably lobsters and shrimp.

The supply of nutrients for plants whose root structure helps support the river delta has been enormously reduced, and now the Mediterranean Sea is slowly encroaching upon and breaking down the land. The electrical potential of the dam's generators has never been realized due to the fact that the reservoir behind the dam is only half full. (It was predicted that it would be filled by 1970, but some experts believe it may never fill because of the porosity of the reservoir floor.) The dam has also been a factor leading to an increase in the debilitating snail-carried disease bilharzia, now affecting about half of Egypt's population. Thus what started out as a worthwhile project in the minds of some has resulted in totally unexpected social, geographic and environmental changes which now must be coped with.

Closer to home, another example of man's upsetting the balance of nature involves the filling-in for real-estate development of the salt marshes of lower Brooklyn and Queens in New York City. Now the Army Corps of Engineers is proposing construction of a $55-million hurricane barrier at the mouth of Jamaica Bay to give the same protection to the land that the salt marsh once provided naturally.

Too many people envision the salt marsh as a biological wasteland and a haven for mosquitoes. In the early development of the coastal United States, salt marshes could at first be bypassed as unsuited for most human purposes. However, as the population expanded and the agrarian society gave way to industry, more pressures came to bear upon the useful development of coastal regions. Today, with approximately eighty-five million

Americans living within one hundred and fifty miles of our east coast, salt marshes are disappearing at a rate of about one per cent per year.

It is true that the flat expanses of grasses seem monotonous and useless, populated as they are with hordes of biting midges, greenhead flies and mosquitoes. But the natural salt marsh-estuarine ecosystem is indispensable to our well-being and is anything but useless.

As a zone between land and sea, marshes protect against the erosional forces of the ocean. A wave breaking over a marsh loses much of the energy that would otherwise act upon the fragile land. Our eastern seaboard is subjected to heavy wave-action from a number of tropical storms and hurricanes that sweep northward each year. A survey of coastal damage after such a storm will invariably reveal that those areas suffering the least destruction were located behind the protective barrier of marshes and sand dunes. Storm damage to the marsh itself is quickly repaired by natural processes.

Salt marshes and their tidal creeks provide food and shelter for many of our birds. Ospreys, marsh hawks, herons, rails, bitterns, grebes, cormorants, marsh wrens, geese and ducks are but a few of the species of wildlife utilizing the marsh system. It is estimated that ducks living within the southern marshes produce upwards of 800,000 ducklings annually.

In addition to birds, the marsh supports huge numbers of other animals. The fiddler crab population alone may exceed 1,000,000 per acre. There can be hundreds of thousands of ribbed mussels in the same area. Also abundant are polychaetes, clams, quahogs, barnacles and snails. In more southerly marshes, diamondback terrapins and alligators are common. Raccoons, mink and beaver may call the marsh their home as well. Countless insects — grasshoppers, crickets, plant hoppers, deer flies, greenhead flies and midges — form a vital link in the food chain.

The marsh can support these large numbers of animals because of its high productivity. The grasses (particularly *Spartina patens* and *alterniflora*), the algae (diatoms and dinoflagellates), and the phytoplankton account for the system's production of organic matter that may approach 10 tons per acre per year. Compare this with the productivity of the continental shelf, which amounts to 1.3 tons per acre per year, or the open-ocean figure of 0.5, and the value of these fragile wetlands takes on increased importance. Even the best of our fertile farmlands will produce only 6 to 7 tons per acre per year, while the average farm produces between 3 and 5 tons. Most of the organic material the marsh produces is not even consumed by the marsh animals, but rather is washed into the tidal estuaries, where it supports large numbers of marine organisms.

It is estimated that seventy per cent of our commercial catch of fish, shrimp, crabs, lobsters and shellfish spend at least part of their lives within the marsh system. Some species are spawned there, while others are simply afforded protection during the process of maturation. Many ocean species feed off the mouths of the estuaries. Nearly 100,000 commercial fishermen depend directly on the marshes to nurture the young of those species that will eventually find their way to our dinner tables.

These same marshes support the multimillion-dollar sport-fishing industry and related activities. Without the marshes there would be less demand for boat-building, fishing equipment, marine repair-yards, restaurants and other enterprises directly or indirectly related to fishing.

The marsh is a storehouse for vital minerals. Because of the mixing action of fresh and salt water, these essential chemical nutrients become trapped within the estuaries. They are then taken up by the phytoplankton and passed through the food chain. At times, industrial effluents or agricultural pesticide runoff will contain heavy metal ions, such as copper. Sediments, particularly clay, on the floor of an estuary have the ability to hold copper ions in loose chemical combination, taking them out of solution when they have exceeded a certain concentration and releasing them when the supply is low. Thus, when not over-loaded by pollution, the marsh acts as a purification system by maintaining a natural chemical balance in the composition of adjacent waters.

Besides supplying the bulk of the organic material produced within the marsh, individual plants have long had economic uses beyond their immediate habitat. Eelgrass (*Zostera marina*) has been extensively used for many years, not only as a fodder for cattle, but also as a fertilizer, fuel, thatching for houses, in the construction of dikes, sound-proofing and insulation in build-ings, as a packing material for fragile glassware, and a mulch in horticulture. It has been a source for soda and salt, stuffing for chairs and mattresses, bedding for domestic animals, as well as food for birds. During World War II, it was used as a substitute for cotton in making nitrocellulose.

In earlier times *Salicornia* was consumed as a pickle and a salad ingredient, while marsh mallow was processed and used as a medicinal herb. According to *Sowerby's English Botany* of 1850, *Spartina alterniflora* was "regularly cut down by the poorer clas-ses and employed by them in lieu of straw or reeds for thatching outhouses, cowsheds etc. and more extensively as litter and sub-sequently as manure. Horses and pigs eat it greedily." The salt-wort, *Salsola Kali*, "was at one time highly valued on account of the quantity of soda it contained, and was collected on the seashore and burned for the use of soap manufacturers. The ashes are known by the name of barilla. Common marsh samphire was used for the same purpose." *Plantago maritima* used to be culti-vated in North Wales because it was "so relished by sheep as food and is considered so good for them — in Wales it is called sheep's herb."

Stachys palustris (marsh woundwort) is recommended in *Gerarde's Herbal* as a vulnerary. We know it was used for the same purpose in ancient times. Sea lavender is still used in dried floral arrangements; medicinally it is utilized for its astringent properties. The dried leaves of germander were powdered and used as a vermifuge.

In Sweden, the panicle (flower cluster) of the common reed *Phragmites communis* was used to dye woolen cloth. Reeds in general were useful in thatching and were in demand by bricklayers. Until the 17th century when bird quills were introduced, reeds were used as writing instruments.

Much research is presently being concentrated on the use of marsh plants as a partial solution to the world's food shortage. One plant receiving particular attention is the cat-tail of the genus *Typha*. Because of this plant's ability to absorb salt, it has been suggested that if cat-tails were planted in coastal areas that are periodically flooded, particularly in the Gulf states of Louisiana and Mississippi, thousands of presently uncultivated acres might become capable of producing a useful crop.

This cat-tail has stirred interest in Russia, and reports indicate that it is used there as a food, as it is elsewhere, notably in India. The Germans have used the fiber in the housing industry as an insulating material, while the French have produced ethyl alcohol from it and have processed the fibers for paper-making.

The first settlers in this country found the Indians making ingenious use of the cat-tail. Squaws used the fluff to pad moccasins and papoose-boards. Mats and baskets were woven from the fiber; dolls and other play-toys were fashioned from the leaves. Indians made use of this remarkable plant throughout the year as a source of food. In the spring, the roots were eaten as a vegetable; during summer, these same roots were made into a soup and could also be made into a syrup as a topping for puddings. During the autumn, a porridge was made from the pollen and some of the roots were stored for roasting during the winter. And at all times, a dressing for wounds was made from cat-tails.

Early coastal settlers in America learned from the Indian how to make cat-tail soup, jelly from the roots and pickles from young shoots. The hollow stems were made into candle-molds, and were also used as torches when dipped into kerosene. Pioneer women used the fluff as fill for quilts.

Birds and animals make use of this plant both as cover and for food. Muskrats will eat the roots, waterfowl will line their nests with the down and the red-winged blackbird will often build its nest directly on the plant.

World War II caused America to make intensified use of its natural raw materials. Cat-tail fluff was processed and used in life-jackets and as stuffing for pillows and cloth dolls. Even our national pastime found a use for the cat-tail fluff — as a stuffing for baseballs.

If need be, American ingenuity can put the seeds of the cat-tail to a number of uses. Oil similar to that made from linseed can be extracted. From this oil, a wax can be produced that may be found useful as a paper-coating. Livestock feed could be made from the remaining pulp. Experiments have shown that cat-tail roots can be ground into a meal that tastes similar to potato flour and makes excellent pastry. Having a high starch content, it can be used like cornstarch in cooking. Ethyl alcohol can be made from the fermented flowers and used for anti-freeze or as an inexpensive industrial solvent. It also can be useful as a substrate in microbiology for the growing of certain molds.

Productivity in cat-tail marshes is exceedingly high. Roots alone can have a yield of up to 150 tons per acre — enough to produce 35 tons of flour. This is over ten times the yield in potato farming. The plant also has a high fiber content. Up to forty per cent of the dry weight of cat-tails can be redeemed as fiber, as compared to only six per cent of other fiber-yielding plants. Each acre of cat-tail can produce a final yield of 4 tons of fiber. While the cat-tail fiber does not have the strength of flax or hemp, it can be employed for many of the same purposes as jute.

In the not too distant future, harvesting of the cat-tail *Typha* may become a highly profitable business, making our present marsh land, if possible, even more worthy of protection.

Many pharmaceutical companies are interested in the possible usefulness in new drugs of substances present in the fauna and flora of the sea. At the present time, with the exception of cod-liver oil, there are few, if any, drug products extracted directly from marine sources commercially sold in the United States. Extracts from a few marine organisms found in marsh estuaries — for example, the common quahog — show anti-tumor properties. Should the active ingredient be identified, it may be possible to synthesize it for use against cancer. Lederle Laboratories has had an active program in marine research since the late 1960's. According to a spokesman, the results are encouraging because the percentage of organisms from the sea containing some kind of biologically active agent is higher than among those in terrestrial habitats.

Salt marshes are dying not from natural processes but from human activities. There is a constant battle between the ever-present "needs" of society and the needs of the multitude of organisms that depend directly or indirectly on the marsh for their sustenance. We have, up to now, too often acted without thorough study of the effects human modifications will have upon any environment, and we are paying for our carelessness. The major threats to estuarine and coastal-zone life may be placed in three categories: destruction of the marshes, destruction of the floor of the estuaries and water pollution.

There is no argument that there are fewer animals, birds, crabs and fish because of poor coastal-zone management. The ocean's productivity is concentrated in the coastal zone, and biological productivity within the marsh estuarine ecosystem is partially dependent upon phosphates and nitrates, which support large populations of phytoplankton that form the base of the food chain. These nutrients are delivered to the marsh as the ocean sweeps over the mud flats and up into the estuaries, leaching the mineral content from the soils of the drainage systems and from the organic waste material accumulated from the river systems.

The dissolved oxygen within the estuary is utilized in the chemical breakdown of organic materials. When organic wastes accumulate faster than they can be decomposed, the dissolved oxygen supply is depleted, thereby eliminating many of the oxygen-demanding organisms, including the indispensable decomposing bacteria itself. When this condition occurs, only certain anaerobic bacteria remain, and these chemically reduce the sulfate in seawater and release poisonous hydrogen sulfide, making life unfit for most organisms. Fortunately, this condition occurs only where water circulation and flow are slow and excessive amounts of waste are introduced into the water. This is the situation partly responsible for the pollution of Lake Erie. Most of our east coast estuarine systems are wide enough at their mouths to permit adequate exchange of seawater and receive a good flushing at each tide. The problem becomes increasingly critical further up the estuary, where the lay of the land may cause sluggish river current and where sea tides cannot reach. And even if we manage to keep our salt marshes healthy, we are dredging and filling too many, to form, typically, a series of peninsulas for house lots where each lucky resident can have his own boat-dock. Invariably, water circulation within these areas is modified to such an extent that it too becomes sluggish, and anaerobic conditions can quickly become established, resulting in odors from hydrogen sulfide and subsequent fish kills.

The dredging of channels in estuaries to accommodate an increasing boat population is common. The silt from such projects is often dumped into the nearest marshland under the guise of improving the area. The dredging can damage marine habitats on the bottom, and the silt placed in temporary suspension will reduce the penetration of sunlight, with consequent deleterious effects on photosynthesis. When the silt eventually settles it then may smother shellfish or bury fish eggs, while the dredged channel may alter the course of water circulation, further changing the entire pattern of life within the estuary.

A number of resources are presently mined in the coastal zone, affecting marine life to a greater or lesser extent. They include oil, natural gas, phosphates, sand, shell and gravel. About seventy-five per cent of our phosphate rocks come from the estuarine zone of the Carolinas, Georgia and Florida. The mining process tears open the salt marsh to expose the mineral beds. The effluent from processing is piped into settling beds, killing all life on the estuarine bottom, with the by-products often being injurious to other wildlife.

It seems clear that tidelands development — residential housing, industrial installations, boat basins and marinas, highways, airports, and recreational areas — damages our marsh estuarine system by dredging and destroying the deeper-water marine habitats on the bottom, at the same time filling in the salt marshes and killing all life there, and, in a final gesture of overkill, polluting the water itself.

Records show that around 1900 there were about forty square miles of marshland in the five boroughs of New York, extending along much of the city's shoreline. Today there are less than six square miles of marsh remaining. It is estimated that since 1940 more than twenty-five per cent of the nation's salt marshes has been destroyed by dredging, landfill and pollution. LaGuardia and Kennedy Airports in New York, San Francisco's International Airport, Boston's Logan Airport, and Washington's National Airport all have been built upon land reclaimed by filling low-lying areas and marshland. Tidal-lagoon developments, such as those being extensively built in Connecticut, near Newark and Atlantic City, New Jersey, and in Delaware, are destroying the bottom, suffocating the marsh, and degrading the quality of the water. The huge housing complex, Co-op City, in East Bronx, New York, and Shea Stadium in Queens were also built at the cost of destroying indispensable marshlands.

Businessmen argue the ratable question — aren't these lands worth more for taxes when they are developed? Some marsh-land real estate in New Jersey commands a premium price of up to $100,000 per acre today. Developers contend that a broader tax base will be of benefit to all. In most cases, this is not true; bigger, more often than not, means higher taxes. Furthermore, any such industrial alternative must be examined for its probable effects in environmental pollution and destruction of all the intangible benefits that brought people to live by the sea in the first place.

Many of the eastern estuaries and marsh systems are affected by water pollution, since the marsh is the repository for most of the wastes carried downstream by the river. As the river meets the estuary, its current slows and deposits its load of domestic sewage and industrial waste (mostly chemicals), upsetting the delicate balance of the natural populations. Many shellfish, particularly clams, concentrate viruses and bacteria from human wastes which can cause illness or death when the shellfish are eaten by man. Health officials must continually check shellfish beds for the presence, and if present, the level of concentration, of the intestinal coliform bacteria. Should the concentration reach a dangerous level, the area is designated as contaminated and closed for the taking of shellfish. In addition, excess sewage from human wastes can, as described earlier, lower the oxygen content of an estuary to such an extent that desirable marine forms will disappear altogether. Industrial wastes often include toxic substances in amounts that exceed the tolerance level of the estuarine inhabitants, also resulting in the total destruction of marine life.

An increasing number of power-generating plants are being constructed along estuaries, which provide the vast amounts of cooling water such installations require. Many of the algae that form the base of the food chain exist in very narrow temperature ranges, and when a large volume of heated water (often exceeding 500,000 gallons per minute) is discharged directly back into the natural environment, the resulting thermal pollution can eliminate many of the species which are fundamental to life in the ecosystem. In addition, heated effluent may interrupt the reproductive cycle of many organisms by causing them to discharge their gametes too soon, resulting in a marked decrease in the numbers of certain species. Ironically, when a power station must be shut down for inspection and repair, the discharge of warm water will not be forthcoming. Those organisms that had succeeded in adjusting to the higher temperature will then probably be eliminated too, especially if the plant is shut down for any length of time.

Adding heated water to an estuary will change the ecology of the entire area. Some species may benefit from the higher temperature, while others will be adversely affected, but in general such action cannot fail to upset the chemical equilibrium within the ecosystem by reducing the amount of dissolved oxygen, reducing light penetration and altering substrate characteristics. The effects are felt not only by the individual species of organisms present, but extend through the many interrelationships that make up the complete ecosystem. To predict the full influence of thermal loading is an almost impossible task.

Much publicity is presently given to offshore oil blowouts and tanker accidents. According to the Environmental Protection Agency, these sources account for less than twenty per cent of the oil introduced into the ocean by man. Most man-induced oil pollution comes from the disposal of waste oil from automobile crankcases and leakage from motors and machinery used on the sea. Only a small percentage is due to natural causes such as leakage from geologic faults in the ocean floor.

Oil dumped at sea may have long-range effects of which we are not now aware. When accidents occur close to land, such as the *Torrey Canyon* disaster of March 1967 off the coast of Cornwall, England, and the Santa Barbara blowout in California in early 1969, we are confronted with the immediacy of the problem.

It has only been since the *Torrey Canyon* accident that oil spills have been extensively studied. We do know that life in the estuaries and salt marshes hangs in delicate balance, and an oil spill, especially of refined oil, will have disastrous, long-term consequences affecting the survival of life in our coastal zone.

Man in his reckless drive toward "improving" life has been destroying it, more often than not. As our population increases, there will be even more intense competition and conflict within our coastal zone.

Historically, legislation pertaining to the environment has been concentrated on conservation of negotiable natural resources or the creation of national parks. However, as far back as 1899, Congress passed the Refuse Act, which prohibited the dumping of refuse and other pollutants into our nation's rivers. Unfortunately, until ten years ago, enforcement was largely neglected. The Water Pollution Control Act (1948) permitted the Federal Government to prosecute polluters. In 1965, the Water Quality Act set standards for the purity of water and empowered the states to take legal action against polluters.

Antipollution planning for river basins, with the Federal Government supplying 50 per cent matching funds for state projects was established by the Clean Waters Restoration Act of 1966. In 1970, after the *Torrey Canyon* and Santa Barbara spills, the Congress passed the Water Quality Improvement Act, designed to control water purity and clean up the nation's waterways. Hitting closer to home, the Act prescribed pollution and sanitation standards for ships and pleasure craft. It also put the oil companies on notice that they were liable for up to $14-million in clean-up costs for oil spillage, set restrictions on thermal pollution from nuclear power plants and developed criteria for measuring the effects of pesticides on the ecology of rivers and streams.

Legislatures at the federal, state and local levels are becoming aware that the delicate wetlands are especially vulnerable to man's activities. All states along the eastern seaboard have legislation controlling, to a greater or lesser extent, any alteration of the coastal zone and its wetlands. About half of our east-coast salt marshes are privately owned, and when the owner is told what he can or cannot do with his own land, the case often becomes a protracted legal battle. In 1973, the American Dredging Company of Philadelphia was enjoined from dumping dredge spoils on its 149 acres of tidal marsh in Gloucester County, New Jersey. The company brought action to challenge the constitutionality of that state's wetlands law and its implementation. Developers are challenging wetland acts in several other states. On September 1, 1973, New York's Tidal Wetlands Act went into effect and within a month builders' associations had filed suit charging it to be unconstitutional. And so the battle goes on.

The future of salt marshes, estuaries and the coastal zone in general looks promising. In 1972, Congress enacted the Coastal Zone Management Act, under whose provisions each state can develop a program for the management, beneficial use, protection and development of its coastal zone to meet its own particular needs. Long before, the Massachusetts legislature had enacted the Coastal Wetlands Protection Act of 1965 in response to potential environmental damage posed by developers of ocean-front properties. And in 1974, a reorganization of the state government established an Executive Office of Environmental Affairs to direct the state's coastal-zone program. Massachusetts, however, has less than two per cent of the east coast's 2,200,000 acres of salt marshes, and we cannot rest easy about the future of the salt marsh until other states follow its enlightened lead.

Indeed, each of us must be concerned with any project that will have environmental consequences. With an energy shortage presently upon us, more pressure can be expected from industry to seek new sources of oil and natural gas, build oil refineries on our coast and drill in our offshore areas. Let us not exchange short-term advantages for undesirable long-term consequences.

Right now. there are enough laws to save our marshes and halt pollution of our environment. What is needed is broad citizen indignation against violators of our natural heritage. We cannot disregard conflicting societal needs, but we can reshape them to conform, as much as possible, with nature's way. As James A. Michener said upon seeing his favorite stream polluted beyond help, " . . . what in all those years had I been doing that was more important than saving a stream?"

Illustrated Appendix
Introduction

Approximately one hundred plant and animal species of the tidal marshes are illustrated in this section. This list is not intended to be all-inclusive but rather to cover the most common indigenous, easy to identify species. Occasional and exotic species have been intentionally omitted.

Salt marsh zonation is based upon Moul, 1973. Plants are illustrated in the zone within which they first appear, beginning with Zone I, the estuary, and proceeding upland. Animals are listed in the phylogenetic sequence.

Accompanying each illustration are the common and scientific names, flowering time and color (for plants), range and size in the metric system (conversion factor, 1 cm. equals 0.39 inches).

Botanical references: Fernald, Merritt L., *Gray's Manual of Botany*, 8th ed. New York: American Book Co., 1950, and Gleason, Henry A., *The New Britton and Brown Illustrated Flora of the Northeastern United States and Adjacent Canada*, New York Botanical Garden.

Zoological references: Miner, Roy Waldo, *Field Book of Seashore Life*, Van Reese Press, New York, 1950, and Smith, Ralph I. (editor), *Keys to Marine Invertebrates of the Woods Hole Region*, Spaulding Co., Inc., Randolph, MA, 1964.

ZONE I: Estuary — sandy or muddy bottom submerged at low tide.

GRASSES

EELGRASS
Zostera marina
Grass-like marine herb. Flowers on spadix hidden in leaf sheath. Grows in shallow water to depths of 30 feet.
Flowers: Summer
s. Greenland to North Carolina

SEAWEEDS

GREEN ALGAE
Enteromorpha intestinalis
Entire east coast

GREEN ALGAE
Enteromorpha erecta
New Brunswick to Long Island

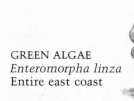

GREEN ALGAE
Enteromorpha linza
Entire east coast

GREEN ALGAE
Codium fragile
New Jersey to Cape Cod

SEA LETTUCE
Ulva lactuca
Entire east coast

ZONE II: Lower border, edge of marsh, along creeks and ditches. Normal tides flood the area twice a day. Spartina alterniflora zone.

GRASSES

SALT-WATER CORD GRASS
Spartina alterniflora
Flowers: July - September
Newfoundland to New Jersey
Size: 0.1 - 2.5 m.

SALT-WATER CORD GRASS
Spartina alterniflora var. *pilosa*
Nova Scotia to North Carolina

SALT-WATER CORD GRASS
Spartina alterniflora var. *glabra*
New York to Florida

GOOSE GRASS
Puccinellia maritima
Flowers: June - July
Nova Scotia to Rhode Island
Size: 1.5 - 10 dm.

SEAWEEDS

BROWN ALGAE
Fucus vesiculosus var. *spiralis*
Along east coast to North Carolina

BROWN ALGAE
Ascophyllum nodosum var. *scorpioides*
Along east coast to New Jersey

FLOWERING PLANTS

DWARF GLASSWORT
Salicornia Bigelovii
Tiny, inconspicuous flowers.
Flowers: August - November
Maine to South Carolina
Size: 1 - 3 dm.

SAMPHIRE
Salicornia europaea
Inconspicuous flowers.
Flowers: August - November
Nova Scotia to Georgia
Size: 1 - 5 dm.

WOODY GLASSWORT
Salicornia virginica
Inconspicuous flowers.
Flowers: August - October
s.e. New Hampshire to South Carolina
Size: 1 - 3 dm.

SEA BLITE (also Zone III, rarely Zone V)
Suaeda maritima
Pale green flowers.
Flowers: July - October
Quebec to Virginia
Size: 0.5 - 4 dm.

SEA BLITE
Suaeda linearis (also Zone III, rarely Zone V)
More erect plant.
s. Maine to Florida and Texas

SEA LAVENDER (also Zones III and V)
Limonium carolinianum
Lavender flowers.
Flowers: July - October
s. New York to Florida
Size: 1.5 - 6 dm.

SEA LAVENDER
Limonium Nashii
Newfoundland to Florida

SALT-MARSH ASTER (also Zone III)
Aster tenuifolius
Pale lavender or white flowers.
Flowers: Late August - October
New Hampshire to Florida
Size: 1.5 - 6 dm.

ZONE III: Lower slope. Area subjected to the higher tides. Spartina patens zone.

GRASSES

SALT-MEADOW GRASS
Spartina patens
Flowers: Late June - October
Newfoundland to Virginia
Size: 1.5 - 8 dm.

SALT-MEADOW GRASS
Spartina patens var. *monogyna*
New Hampshire to Florida

SPIKE GRASS (also Zone V)
Distichlis spicata
Flowers: August - October
Prince Edward Island to Florida
Size: 1 dm. - 1.2 m.

ARROW GRASS (also Zone V)
Triglochin maritima
Flowers: May - August
Labrador to Delaware
Size: Up to 11.5 dm.

SEAWEED

Ascophyllum nodosum var. *scorpioides,* see Zone II

FLOWERING PLANTS

DWARF GLASSWORT, see Zone II

WOODY GLASSWORT, see Zone II

SAMPHIRE, see Zone II

SALT-MARSH ASTER, see Zone II

SEA BLITE, see Zone II, also in V

SEA LAVENDER, see Zone II, also in V

MOCK BISHOP'S WEED (also Zone V)
Ptilimnium capillaceum
White flowers.
Flowers: July - October
s. New England to Florida
Size: 0.1 - 1.9 m.

SALT-MARSH FLEABANE (also Zones V and VI)
Pluchea purpurascens var. *succulenta*
Pink to purple flowers.
Flowers: August - September
s. Maine to Florida
Size: Up to 1.5 m.

SEASIDE GOLDENROD
Solidago sempervirens
Golden yellow flowers.
Flowers: July - November
Newfoundland to New Jersey
Size: 0.2 - 2.5 m.

EARLY SEASIDE PLANTAIN
Plantago juncoides var. *decipiens*
Off-white flowers.
Flowers: June - September
s. Greenland to New Jersey
Size: 5 - 20 cm.

SEASIDE PLANTAIN
Plantago oliganthos
White flowers.
Flowers: July - September
Newfoundland to New Jersey
Size: 5 - 20 cm.

ZONE IV: Pool. Filled with water. Salinity varies with tidal influx or long periods without flooding — may reach salinity of 5.6% or more in summer.

WIDGEON GRASS
Ruppia maritima
Variable cosmopolitan species
Flowers: July - October
Newfoundland to Florida
Size: Leaf blades 2 - 10 cm.

SAGO PONDWEED
Potamogeton pectinatus
Flowers: June - September
Newfoundland to Florida
Size: Stems up to 1 m.

ZONE V: Upper slope. Area subjected to exceptionally high tides. Juncus Gerardi zone.

SEA LAVENDER, see Zones II and III

ARROW GRASS, see Zone III

MOCK BISHOP'S WEED, see Zone III

SALT-MARSH FLEABANE, see Zones III and VI

SEASIDE GOLDENROD, see Zones III and VI

SPIKE GRASS, see Zone III

BLACK GRASS
Juncus Gerardi
Flowers: June - September
Newfoundland to Florida
Size: 1.5 - 8 dm.

BLACK GRASS
Juncus Roemerianus
Flowers: May - October
Maryland to Florida

HALBERD-LEAVED ORACH (also Zone VI)
Atriplex patula var. *hastata*
Green, tiny flowers.
Flowers: July - November
Newfoundland to South Carolina
Size: Up to 1.5 m.

COAST BLITE (also Zone VI)
Chenopodium rubrum
Red, tiny flowers.
Flowers: August - November
Newfoundland to New Jersey
Size: Up to 8 dm.

SAND SPURREY (also Zone VI)
Spergularia marina
Pink flowers.
Flowers: June - October
Quebec to Florida
Size: Prostrate plant

GROUNDSEL TREE (also Zone VI)
Baccharis halimifolia
White or yellow flowers. Dioecious shrub, staminate and pistillate blossoms on separate plants.
Flowers: Late August - October
Maine to Florida
Size: 1 - 3 m.

staminate   pistillate

MARSH ELDER, HIGH TIDE BUSH (also Zone VI)
Iva frutescens var. *oraria*
Greenish white flowers.
Flowers: August - October
Nova Scotia to Virginia
Size: 1.5 - 3.5 m.

SEA MILKWORT (also Zone VI)
Glaux maritima
White, lavender or pink flowers
Flowers: June - July
Gaspé to Virginia

SALT-MARSH BULRUSH
Scirpus maritimus
Flowers: Mid July - October
New Brunswick to Virginia
Size: 0.3 - 1 m.

SEASIDE GERARDIA (also Zone VI)
Gerardia maritima
Pink to rose purple flowers
Flowers: Mid July - September
Nova Scotia to North Carolina
Size: 0.5 - 3 dm.

SEASIDE GERARDIA
Gerardia maritima var. *grandiflora*
Flowers: July - August
Virginia to Florida
Size: 2 - 6 dm.

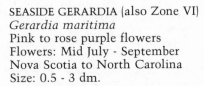

SEABEACH KNOTWEED (also Zone VI)
Polygonum glaucum
Whitish or pink flowers
Flowers: Late July - November
Maine to Georgia
Size: Prostrate plant

ZONE VI: Transition. Upper Border. Area subjected to storm tides only. Upland vegetation taking over and mixed with typical tidal marsh plants.

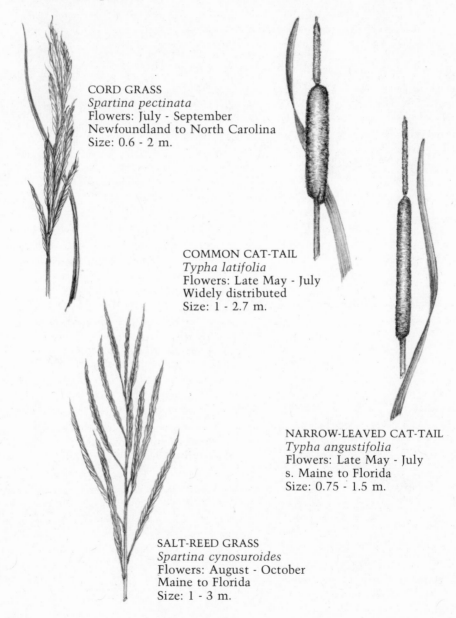

CORD GRASS
Spartina pectinata
Flowers: July - September
Newfoundland to North Carolina
Size: 0.6 - 2 m.

COMMON CAT-TAIL
Typha latifolia
Flowers: Late May - July
Widely distributed
Size: 1 - 2.7 m.

NARROW-LEAVED CAT-TAIL
Typha angustifolia
Flowers: Late May - July
s. Maine to Florida
Size: 0.75 - 1.5 m.

SALT-REED GRASS
Spartina cynosuroides
Flowers: August - October
Maine to Florida
Size: 1 - 3 m.

COMMON REED
Phragmites communis
Flowers: Late July - September
Nova Scotia to Florida
Size: 1.5 - 4 m.

RED FESCUE GRASS
Festuca rubra
Flowers: June - July
Greenland to North Carolina
Size: 0.7 - 9 dm.

SEDGE
Cyperus polystachyos var. *texensis*
Flowers: Late July - October
Maine to Florida
Size: 0.1 - 5 dm.

PANIC GRASS
Panicum longifolium
Flowers: July - October
Nova Scotia to Florida
Size: 0.2 - 1 m.

SWITCHGRASS
Panicum virgatum
Flowers: July - September
Maine to Florida
Size: 0.3 - 2 m.

ORACH
Atriplex patula
Green, tiny flowers.
Flowers: July - November
Newfoundland to North Carolina
Size: Up to 1.5 m.

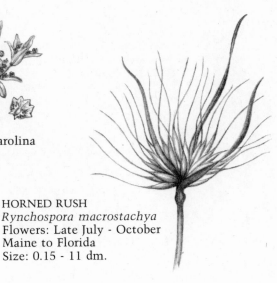

HORNED RUSH
Rynchospora macrostachya
Flowers: Late July - October
Maine to Florida
Size: 0.15 - 11 dm.

SPIKE RUSH
Eleocharis parvula
Flowers: July - October
Newfoundland to Louisiana
Size: culms 1 - 7 cm.

CHAIRMAKER'S RUSH
Scirpus americanus
Flowers: June - September
Newfoundland to Florida
Size: Up to 1.5 m.

SEDGE
Scirpus atrovirens
Flowers: Late June - August
Maine to Georgia
Size: 0.3 - 1.8 m.

TORREY'S RUSH
Scirpus Torreyi
Flowers: July - September
New Brunswick to Long Island
Size: 0.4 - 1.5 m.

SEDGE
Scirpus Olneyi
Flowers: June - September
s. New Hampshire to Florida
Size: 0.5 - 3 m.

SOFT RUSH
Juncus effusus var. *solutus*
Flowers: June - September
Newfoundland to Florida
Size: 0.4 - 2 m.

SEDGE
Scirpus cyperinus
Flowers: August - October
Newfoundland to Florida
Size: Up to 1.5 m.

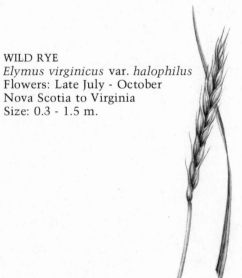

WILD RYE
Elymus virginicus var. *halophilus*
Flowers: Late July - October
Nova Scotia to Virginia
Size: 0.3 - 1.5 m.

RED TOP GRASS
Agrostis alba var. *palustris*
Flowers: June - September
s. Greenland to Virginia
Size: Prostrate, decumbent or erect

SWAMP ROSE MALLOW
Hibiscus palustris
Pink to purple flowers.
Flowers: Late July - early October
Massachusetts to North Carolina
Size: 1 - 2.5 m.

SILVERWEED
Potentilla anserina
Yellow flowers.
Flowers: June - August
Newfoundland to s. New England
Size: Up to 3 dm.

SILVERWEED
Potentilla Egedei var. *groenlandica*
Yellow flowers.
Flowers: May - August
s. Greenland to Long Island

SLENDER-LEAVED GOLDENROD
Solidago tenuifolia
Golden yellow flowers.
Flowers: August - October
Nova Scotia to Virginia
Size: 2.5 - 8 dm.

SEA OR MARSH PINK
Sabatia stellaris
Crimson pink flowers.
Flowers: July - October
Massachusetts to Florida
Size: 0.3 - 5 dm.

LARGE MARSH PINK
Sabatia dodecandra
Pink flowers.
Flowers: July - September
s. Connecticut to Florida
Size: 0.8 - 6 dm.

COMMON SALTWORT
Salsola Kali
Yellow green flowers.
Flowers: July - October
Newfoundland to Georgia
Size: 3 - 8 dm.

CUDWEED
Gnaphalium obtusifolium
White flowers.
Flowers: August - November
Nova Scotia to Florida
Size: 0.1 - 1.5 m.

ROSE
Rosa palustris
Rose flowers.
Flowers: June - August
Nova Scotia to Florida
Size: Up to 2.5 m.

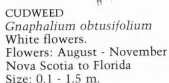

COAST BLITE, see Zone V

HALBERD-LEAVED ORACH, see Zone V

GROUNDSEL TREE, see Zone V

MARSH ELDER, see Zone V

SAND SPURREY, see Zone V

SALT-MARSH FLEABANE, see Zones III and V

SEASIDE GERARDIA, see Zone V

SEASIDE GOLDENROD, see Zones III and V

SEA MILKWORT, see Zone V

SEABEACH KNOTWEED, see Zone V

ANIMALS

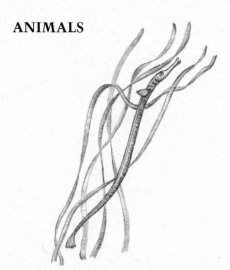

SILVERSIDE
Menidia menidia
Prince Edward Island to Virginia
Size: 7.5+ cm.

SILVERSIDE
Menidia beryllina
New Jersey to Florida
Size: Up to 7.5 cm.

PIPEFISH
Syngnathus fuscus
Gulf of St. Lawrence to South Carolina
Size: Up to 10 - 12 cm.

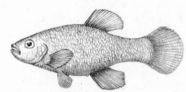

COMMON MUMMICHOG
Fundulus heteroclitus
Canada to Mexico
Size: Up to 12 cm.

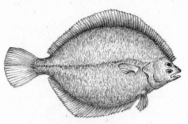

WINTER FLOUNDER
Pseudopleuronectes americanus
Bay of Fundy to Chesapeake Bay
Size: Up to 50 cm.

STRIPED MUMMICHOG
Fundulus majalis
Canada to Florida
Size: Up to 15 cm.

FOURSPINE STICKLEBACK
Apeltes quadracus
Labrador to Virginia
Size: Up to 6 cm.

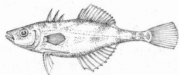

GREEN CRAB
Carcinus maenas
Nova Scotia to Virginia
Size: Up to 7.5 cm.

HORSESHOE CRAB
Limulus polyphemus
Nova Scotia to Florida
Size: Up to 60 cm.

FIDDLER CRAB
Uca minax
From Massachusetts south
Size: Carapace up to 3.81 cm. wide

MARSH FIDDLER CRAB
Uca pugnax
New England to Florida
Size: Carapace up to 2.54 cm. wide

CHINA-BACK FIDDLER CRAB
Uca pugilator
New England to Florida
Size: Carapace up to 3.175 cm. wide

MUD CRAB
Eupanopeus herbstii
Massachusetts to Florida
Size: Carapace up to 2.54 cm. wide

HERMIT CRAB
Pagurus pollicaris
Maine to Florida
Size: Up to 12.7 cm.

HERMIT CRAB
Pagurus longicarpus
Cape Cod to South Carolina
Size: 5.08 - 7.62 cm.

BLUE CRAB
Callinectes sapidus
Cape Cod to Florida
Size: Carapace up to 17.78 - 20.32 cm. wide

LUGWORM
Arenicola marina
Entire east coast
Size: Up to 20.32 cm.

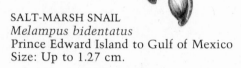

SALT-MARSH SNAIL
Melampus bidentatus
Prince Edward Island to Gulf of Mexico
Size: Up to 1.27 cm.

CLAM WORM
Nereis virens
Labrador to s. New England
Size: Up to 45.72 cm.

CLAM WORM
Nereis pelagica
Greenland to Virginia
Size: Up to 20.32 cm.

CLAM WORM
Nereis limbata
New England to South Carolina
Size: 12.7 - 15.24 cm.

MUD SNAIL
Nassa obsoleta
Nova Scotia to Florida
Size: Up to 2.54 cm.

SPIRORBUS
Spirorbis borealis
Canada to Florida
Size: Up to .32 cm.

OYSTER DRILL
Urosalpinx cinerea
Prince Edward Island to Florida
Size: Up to 2.5 cm.

COMMON PERIWINKLE
Littorina littorea
Canada to New Jersey
Size: 1.91 cm.

NORTHERN ROUGH PERIWINKLE
Littorina saxatilis
Labrador to New Jersey
Size: 1.27 cm.

SOUTHERN PERIWINKLE (lined periwinkle)
Littorina irrorata
New Jersey to Florida
Size: 2.54 cm.

MOON SNAIL
Lunatia heros
Gulf of St. Lawrence to North Carolina
Size: 7.62 - 10.16 cm.

SAND-COLLAR SNAIL
Polinices duplicatus
Massachusetts to Gulf of Mexico
Size: 5.08 - 7.62 cm.

RIBBED MUSSEL
Modiolus demissus
Prince Edward Island to Georgia
Size: Up to 10 cm.

OYSTER
Crassostrea virginica
Gulf of St. Lawrence to Gulf of Mexico
Size: 7.62 - 10.16 cm.

QUAHOG
Mercenaria mercenaria
Gulf of St. Lawrence to Gulf of Mexico
· Size: 7.62+ cm.

SCALLOP
Pecten irradians
Maine to Cape Hatteras
Size: 5.08 - 7.62 cm.

FALSE ANGEL WING
Petricola pholadiformis
Prince Edward Island to West Indies
Size: 5.08 - 6.45 cm.

SCALLOP
Pecten dislocatus
North Carolina to Florida
Size: 2.54 - 5.08 cm.

ANGEL WINGS
Pholas costata
Massachusetts to West Indies
Size: 15.24 - 20.32 cm.

BLUNT RAZOR CLAM
Tagelus plebeius
New England to Florida
Size: Up to 10 cm.

SOFT-SHELL CLAM
Mya arenaria
Arctic to North Carolina
Size: 5.08 - 7.62 cm.

RAZOR CLAM
Ensis directus
Labrador to Florida Keys
Size: 15.24 - 17.78 cm.

CAROLINA MARSH CLAM
Polymesoda caroliniana
North Carolina to Florida
Size: 2.54 cm.

ROCK BARNACLE
Balanus eburneus
Massachusetts to West Indies
Size: Less than 1.27 cm.

ROCK BARNACLE
Balanus balanoides
Arctic Ocean to Delaware
Size: Less than 1.27 cm.

SKELETON SHRIMP
Aeginella longicornis
Maine to Virginia
Size: 2.54 cm.

SAND SHRIMP
Crangon vulgaris
Labrador to Florida
Size: 2.54 - 5.08 cm.

COMMON GRASS SHRIMP
Palaemonetes vulgaris
Cape Cod to Florida
Size: 2.54 cm.

EELGRASS SHRIMP
Virbius zostericola
Cape Cod to New Jersey
Size: Up to 1.91 cm.

SEAWEED HOPPER
Gammarus locusta
Maine to North Carolina
Size: 2.54 cm.

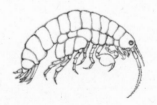

COMMON SAND FLEA
Orchestia platensis
New England to Florida
Size: 3.81 cm.

MARSH CRICKET
Gryllus assimilis
Maine to Delaware
Size: 2.54 cm.

MARSH GRASSHOPPER
Orchelium fidicinum
Massachusetts (occasionally to Florida)
Size: Up to 3.81 cm.

GREENHEAD FLY
Tabanus sp.
Maine to Florida
Size: Up to 1.27 cm.

SALT MARSH MOSQUITO
Aedes sollicitans
New England to Florida
Size: 0.635 cm.

BITING MIDGE
Ceratopogonids
New England to Florida
Size: 0.10 cm.

Index

Page numbers in italic indicate illustrations.

Sparrow, Sharp-tailed, 30. *See also* *Ammospiza caudacuta*

Spartina, harvesting of, 62

Spartina alterniflora, 9, 13, 15, 25, 30, 96. *See also* Grass, Salt-Water Cord; reproduction of, 45, 81; uses of, 82

—*S. alterniflora* var. *glabra, 96*

—*S. alterniflora* var. *pilosa, 96*

Spartina cynosuroides, 60, *104. See also* Grass, Salt-Reed

Spartina patens, See also Grass Salt-Meadow, 8, 14, 15, 21, 30, 62, 63, 84, 98; reproduction of, 45

—*S. patens* var. *monogyna, 98*

Spartina pectinata, 104

Spergularia marina, 43, *101. See also* Spurrey, Sand

Spiranthes cernua, 60. *See also* Ladies' Tresses

Spirorbis, 113

Spirorbis borealis, 113

Spring equinox, 19

Spurrey, Sand, 23, 43, *101. See also* *Spergularia marina*

Stachys palustris, 83. *See also* Woundwort, Marsh

Starfish, 42. *See also Asterias forbesi*

Sterna hirundo, 32. *See also* Tern, Common

Stickleback, Fourspine, 36, *111. See also Apeltes quadracus*

Stridulation, of crickets and grasshoppers, 48

Suaeda linearis, 97

Suaeda maritima, 43, 97. *See also* Blite, Sea

Switchgrass, *105*

Syngnathus fuscus, 111

Tabunus sp., 46, *117. See also* Fly

Tagelus plebeius, 115

Telmatodytes palustris, 30, 33. *See also* Wren, Long-billed Marsh

Tern, Common, 32. *See also Sterna hirundo*

Tidal Wetlands Act of New York (1973), 91

Tides

—semidiurnal, 7

—Spring, 7

Torrey Canyon, 89-90

Totanus melanoleucus, 32. *See also* Yellow-legs, Greater

Triglochin maritima, 99

Typha, economic uses of, 83-85

Typha angustifolia, 104

Typha latifolia, 104

Uca, 29. *See also* Crabs, Fiddler; adaptation for breathing in, 49; claw of, 49; mating behavior of, 49; biological rhythms in, 51

Uca minax, 49, *112*

—*U. pugilator,* 49, *112*

—*U. pugnax,* 49, *112*

Ulva lactuca, 95

Urosalpinx cinerea, 113

Virbius zostericola, 116

Water Pollution Control Act (1948), 90

Water Quality Act (1965), 90

Water Quality Improvement Act (1970), 90

Weasel, 44

Worm, Clam, *113*

Woundwort, Marsh, 83. *See also* *Stachys palustris*

Wren, Long-billed Marsh, 30, 33. *See also Telmatodytes palustris*

Bibliography

Amos, William H., *The Life of the Seashore*, McGraw-Hill Book Co., New York, 1966.

Arnold, Augusta F., *The Sea-Beach at Ebb-Tide*, The Century Company, New York, 1901.

Awake Magazine, *Are Wetlands Worth Preserving*, Vol. 56: No. 3, February 8, 1975.

Bennett, D. W., (editor), *202 Questions for the Endangered Coastal Zone*, Special Publication No. 6, American Littoral Society, 1970.

Berrill, N. J., *The Living Tide*, Fawcett Publications, Inc., Greenwich, Connecticut, 1964.

Buchsbaum, Ralph, *Animals Without Backbones*, The University of Chicago Press, Chicago, 1948.

Carson, Rachel L., *The Sea Around Us*, The New American Library, 1960.

—, *Silent Spring*, (Fawcett Publications, Inc., Greenwich, Connecticut, 1962.)

—, *Under the Sea Wind*, The New American Library, 1941.

Fernald, Merritt Lyndon, *Gray's Manual of Botany*, 8th ed., American Book Co., New York, 1950.

Gates, David A., *A Preliminary Report of Oyster Propagation in Paw Wah Pond and a Pleasant Bay Survey Indicating the Extent and Condition of the Quahog (Venus Mercenaria) Resources*, Orleans, Massachusetts, 1964.

Gates, David A. and H. F. Pettengill, *Ecology of the Oyster Pond Estuarine System*, Chatham, Massachusetts, 1970

—, *Biological Survey of Pleasant Bay*, Chatham, Massachusetts, 1971.

Gleason, Henry A., *The New Britton and Brown Illustrated Flora of the Northeastern United States and Adjacent Canada*, New York Botanical Garden.

Gross, M. Grant, *Oceanography*, Prentice-Hall, Inc., New Jersey, 1972.

Hardwicke, Robert (Publisher), *Sowerby's English Botany*, London, 1863.

Hay, John, *Nature's Year*, Doubleday & Co., Inc., Garden City, New York, 1961.

—, *The Sandy Shore*, The Chatham Press, Inc., Chatham, Massachusetts, 1968.

Hay, John and Peter Farb, *The Atlantic Shore*, Harper and Row Publishers, New York, 1966.

Hitchcock, Stephen W., *Fragile Nurseries of the Sea; Can We Save Our Salt Marshes.*, National Geographic, Vol. 141: No. 6, June, 1972.

Kingsbury, John M., *The Rocky Shore*, The Chatham Press, Inc., Old Greenwich, Connecticut, 1970.

Lutz, Frank E., *Field Book of Insects*, G. P. Putnam's Sons, New York, 1948.

Miller, G. Tyler, Jr., *Living in the Environment: Concepts, Problems and Alternatives*, Wadsworth Publishing Co., Inc., Belmont, California, 1975.

Miner, Roy Waldo, *Field Book of Seashore Life*, Van Rees Press, New York, 1950.

Moul, Edwin T., *Marine Flora and Fauna of the Northeastern United States. Higher Plants of the Marine Fringe*, NOAA Technical Report NMFS CIRC-384, Seattle, Washington, 1973.

Nicol, J. A. Colin, *The Biology of Marine Animals*, Sir Isaac Pitman & Sons, Ltd., London, 1967.

Nixon, S. W. and C. A. Oviatt, *Ecology of a New England Salt Marsh*, University of Rhode Island Reprint No. 16, 1973.

Orr, Robert T., *Animals in Migration*, The Macmillan Co., New York, 1970.

Peterson, Roger Tory, *A Field Guide to the Birds*, Houghton Mifflin Co., Boston, 1947.

Petry, Loren C. and Marcia G. Norman, *A Beachcomber's Botany*, The Chatham Conservation Foundation, Inc., Chatham, Massachusetts, 1968.

Prosser, C. Ladd and Frank A. Brown, Jr., *Comparative Animal Physiology*, W. B. Saunders Co., Philadelphia, 1961.

Smith, Ralph I. (editor), *Keys to Marine Invertebrates of the Woods Hole Region*, Spaulding Co., Inc., Randolph, Massachusetts, 1964.

Smith, Robert L., *Ecology and Field Biology*, Harper and Row Publishers, New York, 1966.

Strahler, Arthur N., *A Geologist's View of Cape Cod*, Natural History Press, New York, 1966.

Teal, John and Mildred, *Life and Death of the Salt Marsh*, Audubon/Ballantine Books Inc., New York, 1969.

Teale, Edwin Way, *Autumn Across America*, Dodd, Mead & Co., New York, 1956.

—, *North With the Spring*, Dodd, Mead & Co., New York, 1957.

Thorson, Gunnar, *Life in the Sea*, McGraw-Hill Book Co., New York, 1973.

Ursin, Michael J., *Life In and Around the Salt Marsh*, Apollo Editions, New York, 1972.

Van Dyke, Henry T., *Our Environment – Pathways to Solution*, Ginn and Co., Lexington, Massachusetts, 1972.

Wagner, Richard N., *Environment and Man*, W. W. Norton & Co., Inc., 1971.